THE "G.O.A.T."

The "Greatest of all time"

DORRANCE
PUBLISHING CO
EST. 1920
PITTSBURGH, PENNSYLVANIA 15238

Dorrance Publishing Co
585 Alpha Drive
Pittsburgh, PA 15238
Visit our website at *www.dorrancebookstore.com*

ISBN: 978-1-6470-2015-6
eISBN: 978-1-6470-2034-7

THE "G.O.A.T."

The "Greatest of all time"

By

The American Thinkers

Dave Ball	Thomas Lifson	Bill Schanefelt
Avi Berkowitz	Jeff Locke	Peter Skurkiss
Mark Deutschle	E. Jeffrey Ludwig	Michael Smith
Brett Graham Fawcett	Lloyd Marcus	Don Sucher
Steve Feinstein	Alexander Markovsky	Rose Tennent
Michael Filozof	Patricia McCarthy	David Clarke
Steve Grammatico	Majid Mohammadi	Gil Gutknecht
Geoffrey P. Hunt	Randolph Parrish	Gina Loudon
Brian C. Joondeph	Richard Jack Rail	William Marshall
Bill King	Caroline Rausch	Wayne Allyn Root
Taylor Lewis	Terry Scambray	Sundance

The complete articles by each of the Above authors comprise the entire contents of this book. Their profound thinking was the inspiration for compiling this anthology on Donald Trump to galvanize "The Case for Reelecting President Donald J. Trump"

An Anthology Compiled by

Felix Tiglao

DEDICATED TO
LILITH

who convinced me to vote for The Donald on November 8, 2016, and to all The Deplorables and fellow Americans who yearn forever to be free.

TABLE OF CONTENTS

PART IV: Policies

PART IV: Politics

Introduction

This book exists because of these amazing wonderful authors whose insights and opinions compel history to preserve their wisdom in book form. They are the stars of this book, each of whom focuses on a unique President and Leader endearing him more to his supporters and perhaps bringing him closer to all other Americans who care. This book would have been more difficult to create if not for the Internet and the digital world. The capacity of the Internet to awaken minds laying bare arguments pro and con so anybody could decide which side to embrace has been marvelous. In this social media world the author has decided to champion President Donald J, Trump. Hereby this collection of writings that crystalizes the essence of his governing style seemingly alien to ordinary politicians – a down to earth no-nonsense business approach; results-oriented, free of political pretensions, bias, fake promises, dubious concessions and compromises almost to the point of appearing undiplomatic. No President has been more fiercely American in modern times and as heroic despite the resistance, obstruction and vilification by the delusional socialist opposition, the absurd globalists, lunatic leftist Hollywood "celebrities" and unhinged liberal media that hurls indignities at him to the extreme, but like a "street fighter" punches back with a knockout blow that freaks them out even more. Yet he has relentlessly prevailed and for one simple reason – the preservation of America. This book should solidify and reinforce his supporters' commitment to re-elect him and perhaps even convince undecideds and unignited liberals to consider joining the movement.

As Clint Eastwood on taking on the Hollywood Libs said " People message me why I stick my neck out for Trump. Why do I tarnish my reputation with a man that's so hated by so many. I don't care how much the media twists what he says. I don't care how bad he looks. I don't care about his sex life. At all. I don't even care that his language skills are not academic. I only look at what he does and what his policies accomplish. I see a booming economy. I see low unemployment rates, I see African Americans back at work. I see American companies that had fled overseas returning home. I see the oldest President staying up till 3 AM in a suit on Air Force One waiting to greet our prisoners returning from Korea. I see China paying attention to him and returning to the negotiating table. I see him strengthening Israel, standing by Netanyahu, recognizing Jerusalem, saying Shehekhianu. I see him freeing Iran from a devastating regime. I see him tough on terrorism. I see a man delivering on every promise he made, not just talking to get votes. I see a lover of America. One who defends his men in uniform stronger than any man I've ever seen. One who is proud of his flag, without feeling sorry, without excuses. I see an American Hero. Let them say what they will. Trump is a Hero, You will see. I love America. He loves America. I love him as our President. No one is without fault. We hired a man to do a job. He has surpassed my expectations in record time, single-handedly fighting the establishment. And he's doing it for free..... stop listening to talking heads. Look at policies. I'm proud to support Trump...."

- H/T (https://www.freedomwatchusa.com)

PART I

WAYNE ALLYN ROOT: Is President Trump "The G.O.A.T.?"

by Assistant Editor May 7, 2019 84

By Wayne Allyn Root

I don't mean to say, "I told you so." But, I told you so.

In almost every column, I celebrate Donald J. Trump and his economic genius. I believe Trump is the greatest economic president in modern American history. Maybe the greatest ever.

Or as the younger generation calls it, "GOAT." (The Greatest of All-Time).

I don't ask you to love his tweets. Or personal attacks. Or every sentence of every Trump speech or interview. Who cares? Let Trump be Trump. Words don't affect your day to day life. What matters is action. And Trump is a man of action.

Trump's words may offend, or irritate, or shock. That's just his way. And mine too. We're both from the streets of New York. We both believe in telling the raw truth- no matter who it offends. We both believe an aggressive, in-your-face offense is the best defense. On the mean streets of New York, that's how you win a street fight. That's how you stay alive.

But what matters is the economy. Your pocketbook. Food on your table. Enough money to take great care of your family. Enough money for a new car or home. Enough money for a nice vacation. That's what most Americans care about. Not a Trump tweet.

The questions that matter above all else, "Are you doing better today than under Obama? Is your life improved? Is your job more secure? Are you more optimistic about the future?" If the answer for each of those questions is "YES," Trump wins by an electoral landslide in 2020.

Well, don't look now, but it's happening exactly as I predicted. Back in early October of 2016, a month before the presidential election that Hillary was expected to win handily, I gave a speech at "The Money Show" in Dallas. It was recorded, by the way.

I predicted a Trump upset victory. But more importantly, I predicted Trump's presidency would produce the greatest economic boom since Reagan. I predicted a jobs boom. A rebirth of high-paying manufacturing jobs. Economic growth of 3% or higher. I predicted one of the great stock market booms in history. I advised buying energy and manufacturing stocks. I predicted America under Trump would become the energy capital of the world. And I predicted Trump's tax cuts and regulation slashing would produce "the Trump golden age of prosperity."

It all came true.

Sure enough, even ultra-liberal CNN now agrees. This past Thursday CNN announced Trump's economic approval rating has soared to an all-time high. CNN's political director David Chalian said, "Here is the Trump card for the president…56% of Americans approve how he's handling the economy. This is the highest number we've ever seen in CNN polling…"

At the same time, Gallop reported 56% of Americans rate their economic health as excellent or good. Only 15% rate it as poor. Where I come from 56% to 15% is a landslide.

This was all before the Labor Department reported on Friday 263,000 new jobs were created in April, far above expectations. Unemployment hit 3.6%, the lowest since 1969. Can you even remember 1969? I can't either.

Even better news: Unemployment for women dropped to the lowest since 1953. And Hispanic unemployment dropped to the lowest in history. I can't wait for Nancy Pelosi, Chuck Schumer and Alexandria Ocasio Cortez to explain why this is a bad thing.

Trust me, Trump just guaranteed himself the largest share of the Hispanic vote for any Republican in history.

At the same time, the Fed announced despite fast economic growth and fast job growth, there is little to no inflation. Trump has produced "the Goldilocks economy." It's not too small, not too big, not too fast, not too slow. It's just right.

Trump may actually be the G.O.A.T. (the greatest of all-time).

https://newsmax.com/article/is_president_trump_the_g.o.a.t.?
Published with permission from Wayne Allyn Root.

PART II:
THE DOCTRINE

American Thinker

Is Donald Trump More Conservative Than Conservatives?

By Brett Graham Fawcett
August 22, 2016

"**I.**

The backlash against Donald Trump from a lot of groups is predictable, but one of the more interesting cases of this reaction is from the conservative intelligentsia.

Trump's sins against conservatism are, they tell us, that he is not pro-liberty enough. His proposals, from the infamous wall to a potential tax on imported goods, all smack of statism, rather than the crystalline purity of the free market and all its attendant liberties.

But what this criticism conceals is the fact that broadly speaking, there are two major strains, or streams, of tradition within what is commonly called "conservatism." One may be called the "capitalist" strain, which extols liberty as the highest good in and of itself. The other may perhaps be called the "localist" tradition, which views liberty as a means rather than an end, and not always a good in itself. The localist tradition extols the family, the community, and, by extension, the nation as the highest social good, with liberty as its handmaid.

In this article, I will not defend either of these two traditions. Nevertheless, I will argue that, for better or for worse, the localist tradition is the more "original" conservatism, and the Trump phenomenon represents a kind of conservatism *within* conservatism.

Ironically, the thinker who best explains this kind of American First-ism, I think, is actually a Canadian.

In 1965, George Parkin Grant published *Lament for a Nation: The Defeat of Canadian Nationalism*. For this, Grant was considered the father of Canadian nationalism, but arguably his principles can be used to explain the intellectual underpinnings of the American nationalism of Trump and his supporters.

Grant, a Platonist philosopher of religion, believed that a form of political loyalty is necessary for the good life; it is an allegiance that draws the individual out of himself toward a higher good. But Canada was in danger, as were all other nations, of being absorbed into a homogenizing super-state. This homogenization was being achieved by the proliferation of technology: because technology encourages the achievement of desires, it trained the mind to value will over anything else, including any political or moral boundaries, which Grant called the essence of "liberalism": a belief that individual liberty is the highest good. Thus, a liberal cosmopolitanism was eroding all sense of national loyalty in favor of a globalism that would necessarily be a Huxleyan tyranny and would make the good life impossible.

The only way to arrest this technological homogenization, Grant believed, was through a level of government control of the economy to stop the effects of global capitalism, and this was something the Conservative Party of Canada had once held to. When Canada first came into existence, the Conservatives implemented a protectionist National Policy, applying high tariffs on imported goods in order to protect Canadian industry. This policy was gutted by the Liberals, and eventually, much to Grant's chagrin, "conservatives" began to adopt free-market dogma (which was really right-wing liberalism) instead of historic Toryism.

III.

We will come back to the National Policy, but for now, it is worth stressing that Grant did indeed represent an older conservatism. Ralph Nader has chronicled the anti-capitalism of the early American conservative movement, such as the Southern Agrarians. Notably, Nader has also said some approving things about Trump for standing athwart the capitalist establishment.

Mainstream conservatism ended up rejecting this kind of Luddite nostalgia. William F. Buckley, Jr. himself, quoting Whittaker Chambers, remarked that a conservatism that rejects industrialism in the age of the machine is little more than "literary whimsy." Moreover, this kind of localist, anti-capitalist rhetoric was admittedly used as justification for fascism and anti-Semitism. But identifying Trump as a fascist is approaching him from the wrong angle. There is a precedent for his thinking much closer to home.

The National Policy of Canada took its influence from the "National System" or the "American System," or what used to be called the American School of Economics, since it was the economic program that dominated the country until the 1970s. To summarize this system, America's strength and independence should be assured by a strong, well equipped standing army, by protective tariffs, and by subsidies into roads and canals. All of this was inspired by the German economist Friedrich List, who rejected Adam Smith's economic philosophy of individual interest in favor of a philosophy of national or communal interest.

Now, this is almost exactly Trump's platform, and it is exactly why he is denounced as a bad conservative: because of all the spending he is proposing, for following List rather than Smith. Obviously, strengthening the military is a prominent aspect of his platform, but less well-reported on is his suggestion of tariffs to protect American industry and his intention to increase spending on infrastructure. Moreover, he wishes to subsidize American industries such as ethanol, completely counter to the ruthless logic of the free market, simply because it is American. *This* is how Trump's now iconic slogan must be understood; this is the perceived one-time greatness of America he wishes to restore.

V.

It must be said frankly that the instincts behind Trump's policies and the instincts behind the Trump *phenomenon* have to be distinguished. Timothy Cardinal Dolan is certainly correct when he recognizes aspects of the old anti-Catholic American nativism flaring up amongst the fervor of Trump's supporters.

But they must be distinguished from Trump himself, who, it should be noted, has appointed two Catholics, Steven K. Bannon and Kellyanne Conway, to run his campaign. Moreover, not only is Trump in favor of legal immigration, but beneath his smoldering rhetoric against all the criminality illegal immigration ushers in (understandable when one considers MS-13), he has advocated a plan whereby undocumented immigrants, upon being deported, would have a fast-tracked reapplication process. Trump thus defends a "path to citizenship" not dissimilar to the policy of "earned legalization" advocated by the U.S. Catholic bishops, who, in their words, "accept the legitimate role of the U.S. government in intercepting unauthorized migrants who attempt to travel to the United States."

VI.

None of this is an endorsement of Trump; none of this is a defense of any of these policies. But it is important for self-identified conservatives, especially those who are baffled by conservative support for Trump, to understand the intellectual and philosophical heritage that gave rise to his campaign and his candidacy.

It may be surprising that in this time of fierce social conflict, the Republicans did not gravitate toward a conventional culture warrior like Ted Cruz, and many are flabbergasted that Evangelicals seem to be flocking to a crude, multiply divorced media mogul like Trump (forgetting, perhaps, that the Bible is full of examples of morally compromised leaders who nevertheless accomplish great things). But someone like George Grant gives us an insight into a sentiment that holds that traditional morality cannot be preserved if the tradition-bearing *com-*

munity is not. It is clear that, to many, the appeal of Trump is that they think he will protect that community.

Say what you will about that belief, but it is certainly conservative."

-H/T Brett Graham Fawcett

https://www.americanthinker.com/.../**is_donald_trump_more_co nservative_ than_conservatives**.html
Published with permission from the American Thinker.

Sundance

The Professional Political Machine Says: "Donald Trump is Not Conservative" (Part 1)...

Posted on January 10, 2016 by sundance

"PART I – The professional political class continue to say candidate Donald J Trump is not conservative enough on his positions. Various voices proclaim ownership of some arbitrary defining litmus test – *that apparently moves depending on the definition of the person making the proclamation.*

... so let's cut through the BS and take a look at the issues.

♦   **On Immigration** – Donald Trump is the originator of the entire immigration debate platform. His position is outlined HERE, and is the ONLY candidate who proposed to build a wall, deport those who are here illegally, and use existing law to ensure enforcement mechanisms are deployed to stop the illegal influx.

Including a critical proposal to use federal banking and money services regulations (wire transfer rules to Mexico) to aid in creating an incentive to become compliant with immigration law.

Trump has proposed removing executive restrictions on deportation through ICE (Immigration and Customs Enforcement) officers, allowing immediate deportation for undocumented illegal aliens. The media call this "the deportation force".

In addition, candidate Trump has proposed an end to the concept of "birthright citizenship" or "anchor babies", which has never been adjudicated as a valid method for attaining citizenship and most legal minds believe is nonsense. Candidate Ted Cruz believes "anchor babies" are U.S. citizens at birth.

No-one is more "conservative" on Immigration than Donald J Trump.

- **On Second Amendment** – Donald Trump has proposed the end of "gun-free zones" on military bases and federal properties, allowing the individual states to determine where citizens are allowed to carry firearms. Full Policy Outline HERE.

In addition, Trump has proposed that all states observe reciprocity with regard to concealed carry permits. Meaning anyone can travel anywhere in the country using their concealed carry permit from their home state. Essentially the same reciprocal arrangement and consideration that applies to driver's licenses.

No-one is more "conservative" on Second Amendment Rights.

- **On Taxes** – Donald Trump has a fully outlined tax policy available HERE. Which includes provisions to stop corporate inversion and return U.S. corporate monetary assets to the U.S. without penalty.

Additionally, the tax rates are substantially reformed and streamlined where income tax payments do not begin until the wage earner surpasses $50,000 in annual income. Trump is also proposing that Wall Street Hedge Fund operators cannot use capital gains rates to avoid their income tax bracket which would ensure that very wealthy individuals cannot use loopholes and multiple accounting gimmicks to remove their own tax liability.

The Trump Tax proposal is a populist approach to improving the "middle class" wage earner and providing upward mobility. However, it is also one small part of a larger economic plan that unleashes economic growth.

- **On Trade** – Candidate Trump folds the Tax Proposal into a more broad America-First economic policy through renegotiated trade deals. The policy on China Trade specifically is available HERE.

Candidate Trump is against the Obama negotiated Trans-Pacific Trade Deal which has the blessing of congress (thanks to Ted Cruz and Trade Promotion Authority) and approvals of Wall Street and the U.S. Chamber of Commerce (crony capitalists).

Candidate Trump was the first to stand against TPP and also

boldly propose that the 20-year-old NAFTA (North American Free Trade Alliance) trade treaties should be renegotiated to ensure the Mexican trade economy is no longer able to skirt manufacturing rules and create outsourced jobs and manufacturing from the U.S.

The Trump platform on trade is "fair deals, and fair markets" that benefit U.S. jobs and the U.S. economy, not just one-way free-market arrangements.

No-One is more "conservative" on U.S. Jobs, Trade or the U.S. economy.

◆ **On Energy Policy** – Candidate Trump supports the Keystone oil Pipeline a collaborative effort between the U.S. and Canada. In addition, Trump supports broad U.S. energy resource development to include execution of, and development of, U.S. Oil Leases in all regions of fossil fuel development.

Trump has proposed continued investment and exploration of "clean coal" technology using the vast coal mine resources in the Appalachian Range throughout West Virginia and into Pennsylvania. Trump has proposed energy export leverage (oil, coal, natural gas) as part of the larger Trade-deal packages.

The U.S. can negotiate a resurgence of U.S. manufacturing with lower fully developed energy costs, a competitive advantage; and simultaneously our abundant resources in energy fuels also provide trade leverage (standards and tariffs) through energy export.

With a fully utilized energy sector, the U.S. can also use the accompanying economic growth to invest in alternative resource development such as nuclear, solar and wind. The costs of alternative fuel research and development become underwritten by the expansive use of current resources.

No-one is more "conservative" *and smart* on fully developed energy use.

◆ **On Education** – Candidate Trump has clearly stated his opposition to Federal Common Core programs which mandate education policy from bureaucrats in Washington DC. Trump does not believe in federal control of education and has clearly and succinctly stated that educational standards should be developed, and carried out, by those closest to the schools, parents and teachers.

Trump does not, and will not, support programs like "race to the top" (Obama), or "no child left behind (G.W. Bush). Instead, he prefers decisions regarding standards to be made by individual states and local communities.

Candidate Trump, unlike Jeb Bush, would not support withholding funds from states, as blackmail to insure common core is used.

* **On Military** – Candidate Donald Trump has proposed a similar Reagan-era approach toward rebuilding the U.S. Military apparatus as a professional fighting force. Throughout Trump's campaign, he has highlighted his intention to strengthen the U.S. modern military assets and build a comprehensive modern-era military.

However, candidate Trump views the U.S. military as a national force, and nation's military, and runs counter to modern military-industrial complex (neo-con) approach by eliminating military "outsourcing" or contractors (ex Blackwater).

Trump believes the collaborative private/government sector military partnership should be limited to the modernization of equipment and material (research and development), and never the deployment of soldiers or U.S. fighting forces.

Trump has expressed that American sons and daughters who serve in the military should be commanded by the best military and civilian leadership possible. However, our soldiers should never be deployed through the use of private contractors who operate within a grey area, and whose objectives can become detached and end up serving their own best interests.

Candidate Donald Trump is nationally loyal to U.S. interests and extraordinarily "conservative" with reverence, to the traditions of the U.S. military. (Reagan approach)

* **On Foreign Policy** – Donald J Trump is neither an "isolationist" nor an "interventionist". Instead, as Trump has outlined numerous times, our approach to foreign affairs should always be through the prism of U.S. interests first and foremost.

Lead when prudent, support when needed.

Two Current Examples include:

> • *Syria – Monitor closely, but allow Russia to fight ISIS in Syria to the extent their interests do not conflict with our own. Build an international coalition to make a geographic "safe zone" within Syria where allied forces can protect Syrian refugees on the ground from any ISIS attacks – open direct lines of communication with Bashir Assad and negotiate with Vladimir Putin to use Russia's military deployment and ensure a stable transitional government for the people of Syria.*

> • *Ukraine – Monitor closely, support Germany and European allies in their efforts to work through the conflict with Russia and Ukraine. Any "coalition development or intervention" must come from Germany as lead, with our support. Germany is the regional economic powerhouse and nation dependent on Russian energy use.*

Our actions within the global community should be well known, well defined, exceptionally forthright, direct, strong and unequivocal. The American people should know what we are doing internationally, why we are doing it, and be able to see what value there is in our endeavors. It is important to return to an era of clarity.

While Donald Trump's foreign policy approach might not make the interventionist crowd (Neo-cons) happy, it will also not make the isolationist crowd (libertarians) happy. The influence of the U.S. is only as strong as our ability to have our own national house in order.

After years of poor investment in U.S. infrastructure, lack of expansive economic development, burdensome regulations and trade/manufacturing deals antithetical to the U.S. middle class – Trumps proposals to look inward, put America first, and spend time polishing the lens on the 'beacon of freedom', are prudent, necessary and wise.

Simply, lets…

"Make America Great Again!"

If that's not conservative enough for you, I honestly don't know what could be.."

Sundance

" The Professional Political Machine Says: "Donald Trump is Not Conservative" (Part 2)…

Posted on January 11, 2016 by sundance

Part 2 – The professional political class continues to say candidate Donald J Trump is not conservative enough on his positions. Various voices proclaim ownership of some arbitrary defining litmus test – *that apparently moves depending on the definition of the person making the proclamation.*

… so let's cut through the BS and take a look at the issues.

Part 1 reviewed the Trump Policies on   Immigration   The Second Amendment   Taxes   Trade   Energy Policy   Education   Military and Foreign Policy

So we continue exploring the Trump Doctrine with:

 ♦ **Healthcare Policy** – While Donald Trump has not laid out a formal Healthcare policy we are able to assemble the outline with a review of his 2015 verbal comments and proposals (interviews) regarding ObamaCare and Health Care Reform.

Candidate Trump has committed to a full repeal of ObamaCare with a replacement policy proposal consisting of patient-centered, market-based reform. Trump has outlined a desire to remove the state regulatory barriers on healthcare insurance exchanges allowing insurance companies to present an insurance product across state lines, a market-based approach.

Businesses and individuals would be able to purchase health insurance from any company regardless of origination state. All insurance companies would be able to compete for and offer insurance coverage toward, the consumer and/or business in any state.

However, Trump has also proposed federal guidelines, rules, to ensure the financial solvency of any health insurance company. Any healthcare insurance provider would have to pass regulatory and compliance financial "stress tests" and retain financial reserves as established by federal regulatory agencies. A similar approval and regulatory program is currently in place for financial/banking services to eliminate risk.

Each insurance provider would also be required to pay a fee, into a federally controlled risk pool established in the event any single provider is unable to meet their policy obligations. The collection of these fees eliminates the risk of a taxpayer-funded bailout if an insurance carrier becomes insolvent. This process also allows insurance regulators to keep the market flush with multiple competitive carriers eliminating a too big to fail monopoly by any individual carrier. (Think Hurricane Insurance Programs).

This market approach would open the health insurance markets to competitive pricing and allow consumers to tailor their coverage to their individual needs. The insurance product is offered by the insurance company, the individual has choices and options.

Low-income healthcare coverage is continued through the use of the current Medicaid services program and is provided as a subsidy or voucher to the insured customer. In addition, Trump is open to "health savings accounts" so long as the account itself is controlled by the individual and catastrophic insurance coverage is included as part of the overall program.

Candidate Trump has also proposed retention of the mandated "pre-existing coverage" rule insuring that people cannot be denied entry into the market based on pre-existing conditions. However, unlike ObamaCare, Trump is also proposing a "High-Risk Pool" subsidy for those who have extensive and long-term medical issues.

The long-term medical coverage subsidy for high-risk patients would be administered through the existing Medicaid and medicare process; the difference becomes the amount of the subsidy which would be based on the individual or family income level, and extent of the coverage needed.

◆ **On Veteran Healthcare (VA)** – Donald Trump has recommended a complete overhaul of the Veterans Assistance programs. – Policy Outline HERE –

"Under a Trump Administration, <u>all</u> veterans eligible for VA health care can bring their veteran's ID card to <u>any</u> doctor or care facility that accepts Medicare to get the care they need <u>immediately</u>. Our veterans have earned the freedom to choose better or more convenient care from the doctor and facility of their choice. The power to choose will stop the wait time backlogs and force the VA to improve and compete if the department wants to keep receiving veterans' healthcare dollars. The VA will become more responsive to veterans, develop more efficient systems, and improve the quality of care because it will have no other choice".

◆ **On Social Security** – Unlike many candidates, Donald Trump is NOT calling for rapid or wholesale changes to the current Social Security program. With the single caveat of "high-income retirees" (over $250k annually), which Trump is open to negotiating on, candidate Trump does not consider these programs as "entitlements". The American people pay into them, and the federal government has an obligation to fulfill the promises made upon collection.

To fully understand how Donald Trump views the solvency of Social Security, you must understand his economic model and how it outlines growth.

The issue with Social Security, as viewed by Trump, is more of an issue with receipts and expenditures. If the aggregate U.S. economy is growing by a factor larger than the distribution needed to fulfill its obligations then no wholesale change on expenditure is needed. The focus needs to be on continued and successful economic growth.

What you will find in all of Donald Trump's positions is a paradigm shift he necessarily understands **must take place** in order to accomplish the long-term goals for the U.S. citizen as it relates to "entitlements" or "structural benefits".

All other candidates are beginning their policy proposals with a fundamentally divergent perception of the U.S. economy. They are working with and retaining the outlook of, a U.S. economy based on "services"; a service-based economic model.

While this economic path has been created by decades-old U.S. policy and is ultimately the only historical economic path now taught in school, Trump intends to change the course entirely. Because so many shifts -policy nudges- have taken place in the past several decades, few academics and even fewer MSM observers, are able to understand how to get off this path and chart a better course.

Candidate Trump is proposing less dependence on foreign companies for cheap goods, (the cornerstone of a service economy) and a return to a more balanced U.S. larger economic model where the manufacturing and production base can be re-established *and competitive* based on American entrepreneurship and innovation.

No other economy in the world innovates like the U.S.A, Trump sees this as a key advantage across all industry – including manufacturing.

The benefit of cheap overseas labor, which is considered a global market disadvantage for the U.S., is offset by utilizing innovation and energy independence.

The third highest variable cost of goods beyond raw materials first, labor second, is energy. If the U.S. energy sector is unleashed -and fully developed- the manufacturing price of any given product will allow for global trade competition even with higher U.S. wage prices.

In addition, the U.S. has a key strategic advantage with raw manufacturing materials such as iron ore, coal, steel, precious metals and vast mineral assets which are needed in most new modern era manufacturing. Trump proposes we stop selling these valuable national assets to countries we compete against – they belong to the American people, they should be used for the benefit of American citizens. Period.

EXAMPLE: Currently China buys and recycles our heavy (steel) and light (aluminum) metal products (for pennies on the original manufacturing dollar) and then uses those metals to reproduce manufactured goods for sale back to the U.S. – Donald Trump is proposing we do the manufacturing ourselves with the utilization of our own resources; and we use the leverage from *any sales of these raw materials* in our international trade agreements.

When you combine FULL resource development (in a modern era) with the removal of over-burdensome regulatory and compliance systems, necessarily filled with enormous bureaucratic costs, Donald Trump feels we can lower the cost of production and be globally competitive. In essence, Trump changes the economic paradigm, and we no longer become a dependent nation relying on a service-driven economy.

In addition, an unquantifiable benefit comes from investment, where the smart money play -to get increased return on investment- becomes putting capital INTO the U.S. economy, instead of purchasing foreign stocks.

With all of the above opportunities in mind, this is how we get on the pathway to rebuilding our national infrastructure. The demand for labor increases, and as a consequence so too does the U.S. wage rate which has been stagnant (or non-existent) for the past three decades.

As the wage rate increases, and as the economy expands, the governmental dependency model is reshaped and simultaneously receipts to the U.S. treasury improve. More money into the U.S Treasury and less dependence on welfare programs have a combined exponential impact. You gain a dollar and have no need to spend a dollar. That is how the SSI and safety net programs are saved under President Trump.

When you elevate your economic thinking you begin to see that all of the "entitlements" or expenditures become more affordable with an economy that is fully functional. As the GDP of the U.S. expands, so does our ability to meet the growing need of the retiring U.S. worker. We stop thinking about how to best divide a limited economic pie and begin thinking about how many more economic pies we can create.

Simply put, we begin to....

...Make America Great Again!

Again, if that's not a classic approach to being fiscally conservative and solvent, I don't know what is."

H/T Sundance

" The Fundamentals of MAGAnomics....

Posted on July 27, 2018 by sundance

Against the backdrop of MAGAnomic success, many people (some young some old) are beginning to engage in questions of decades-old economic *assumptions*. Consider me thrilled at the possibility of a generational economic awakening.

Toward that end, here's another repost from 2016 to gain an understanding of the fundamentals behind President Trump's MAGAnomic policies. God Bless Main Street!

NOVEMBER 2016 – As we all begin to filter the impact of a historic Donald Trump victory, perhaps it is important to remind ourselves what should be the primary filter for perspective.

...the economics.

For the first time in many decades, the chief executive of the United States will walk into office concerned about the long-term financial stability of the United States. For the first time ever, a titan of American Main Street is going to be in the oval office. **Do not** downplay the significance of this aspect. Money makes the world go 'round.

Every single global leader and politician is reviewing the U.S. election through their own domestic financial prisms. Rule #1 – Everything is about the money. Rule #2 – Everything is about the money. Rule #3 – when pondering any information broadcast by corporate media about a global Trump effect, refer back to the prior two rules.

Donald Trump is 100% pure MAIN STREET, never doubt that. Trump's macroeconomic DNA outlook is comprised of American business interests at a micro-cellular level. Senate Leader Mitch McConnell et al will be dispatched immediately if he attempts to bring his big Wall Street/K-Street lobbying friends into the Trump economic equation.

For the sake of brevity, we're going to accept that most readers here are familiar with who funds and directs Mitt Romney, Paul Ryan, Jeb Bush, John McCain, Mitch McConnell, and in larger more consequential measures – the DC UniParty legislative team in charge of U.S. Policy, ie. *Wall street.*

During the January 2016 South Carolina debate, and in response to Trump pointing out a necessary shift in trade position (a shift to put American interests first – a shift to stop the dependency on cheap imported goods – a shift to use China's dependency on access to our market to OUR advantage), Jeb Bush came back with an example of Boeing manufacturing.

Donald Trump responded to Jeb's *Boeing example* and pointed out China is forcing Boeing to open a manufacturing plant in China. As would be typical from a candidate who is unfamiliar and poorly briefed on the issue, Jeb Bush looked back incredulously and said:

"C'mon man"...

There we saw it.

Right there was the disconnect.

However, almost everyone missed it.

There, in that exact moment, was the spotlight upon all that is wrong with a professional political class; globalists **dependent on Wall Street best interest for their talking points.**

Donald Trump was 100% correct.

But the issue is bigger.

Not only is China demanding Boeing open a plant in China, the intent of such a plant provides an opportunity to explain why Trump, and his approach, is vitally important – and time is wasting.

China is refusing to trade with (buy) Boeing products if the company does not move. Why? It's not about putting Chinese people to work, it's about China importing their research and development, Boeing's production secrets, into their country so they can learn, steal and begin to manufacture their own airliners.

This is just how China works.

In time, Comac, a state-owned, Shanghai-based aerospace company will then use the production secrets they have stolen, produce their own airliners, kick out Boeing, undercut the market, and sell cheaper manufactured airplanes to the global economy.

Boeing, the great American company that Jeb Bush thinks they are, becomes yet another notch on the Asian market belt.

All of those Boeing workers, those high-wage industrial skill jobs that support the American middle class, yeah – those jobs lost. And the cycle continues.

Of course, Wall Street will be invested in the cheaper Chinese aerospace manufacturing company Comac, as it emerges as a manufacturing power.

This reality within this story is a peek into the future of the fundamental disconnect between Wall Street (*grows again*) and Main Street (*lost jobs/wages*). The reality within this example is exactly what has taken place over the past three decades.

Wall Street entities like Goldman Sachs will be fine. Ted and Heidi Cruz will be fine; Jeb Bush, Marco Rubio, Nikki Haley, Carly Fiorina, Mitt Romney, John Kasich will also be fine – it's middle America who suffers.

The economic consequence, yet again, creates disparity between those insulated by Wall Street and the rest of the U.S. This is how our current oligarchy is growing out of control.

And so they, as professional politicians, will propose solutions –

their solutions. However, their solutions are actually the preferred solutions of their campaign contributors, ie. Wall Street. The same Wall Street that funds lobbyists, like the U.S. Chamber of Commerce, to set the economic legislative priorities of Congress.

Meanwhile, the non-import market, your visit to the grocery store, food, energy, etc. sees prices increasing. This is what happens when a production economy becomes a service economy.

In 1984 a name brand polo shirt would cost around $45, a really good 26 TV around $600 to $1,000, a decent couch $1500, and a pair of name brand sneakers around $100. However, eggs (.49), milk ($1.79 gal), and store bread (2 loaves for $1).

Electric bill $100, water bill $20, phone bill $50.

In 2016 an imported name-brand polo costs around $20, a really good 42 TV $300 to $400, a couch for $500 and a pair of sneakers $50 – All imported, all Asian, all about half of what they cost in 1984.

However, eggs ($1.99), Milk ($4.50+), and store bread ($2+ each). All domestic products and all double or triple 1984. Electric bill $250, Water bill $100, phone bill $100+. Again domestic consumables, again double, triple or even more.

We consume and spend more on domestic goods such as food, energy, fuel than we do purchasing imported durable goods. As a consequence, depending on lifestyle, the net out-of-pocket is essentially the same to a little more.

However, the income opportunity, the jobs, the good-paying jobs, well, those are gone because the durables are no longer part of the domestic production.

To keep the unemployed pitchforks at bay, government policy (now directed by Wall Street globalists and multinational corporations) subsidize the income gap. Ergo EBT, WIC, and food stamp assistance necessarily increasing.

The pitchforks are dropped, but economic independence turns to dependence. With government policy adjusted accordingly – **deficits necessarily explode**. Stopping those deficits would require an actual budget. There hasn't been a federal budget since '07.... "Omnibus",... Sound familiar?

Yes, under Donald Trump's proposal the cost of "durable" goods -at least those we import- will increase. Your iPhone might cost $800 instead of $600. However, the North Carolina apparel, clothing and furniture manufacturing market will have an opportunity to revitalize – and with it, jobs, people as the tailors and the custom wood furniture makers would have the opportunity to thrive again with their creations.

There's going to be a period of pain as U.S. manufacturing finds it's footing and begins to restart. However, in the longer term, it's a shift from "dependency" to "independence".

Those who were fully matriculated independent adults prior to 1984 know exactly what needs to be done.

Freedom is dependent upon it.

♦ **On Social Security** – Unlike many candidates Donald Trump is **NOT** calling for rapid or wholesale changes to the current Social Security program, and there's a very good reason why he's the only candidate not proposing wholesale changes.

With the single caveat of "high-income retirees" (over $250k annually), which Trump is open to negotiating on, candidate Trump does not consider these programs as "entitlements". The American people pay into them, and the federal government has an obligation to fulfill the promises made upon collection.

To fully understand how Donald Trump views the solvency of Social Security, you must again understand his economic model and how it outlines growth.

The issue with Social Security, as viewed by Trump, is more of an issue with receipts and expenditures. If the aggregate U.S. economy is growing by a factor larger than the distribution needed to fulfill its entitlement obligations then no wholesale change on expenditure is needed. The focus needs to be on continued and successful economic growth.

What you will find in all of Donald Trump's positions, is a paradigm shift he necessarily understands **must take place** in order to accomplish the long-term goals for the U.S. citizen as it relates to "entitlements" or "structural benefits".

All other candidates are beginning their policy proposals with a fundamentally divergent perception of the U.S. economy. They are working with and retaining the outlook of, a U.S. economy based on "services"; a service-based economic model.

While this economic path has been created by decades-old U.S. policy and is ultimately the only historical economic path now taught in school, Trump intends to change the course entirely.

Because so many shifts -policy nudges- have taken place in the past several decades, few academics and even fewer MSM observers, are able to understand how to get off this path and chart a better course.

Candidate Trump is proposing less dependence on foreign companies for cheap goods, (the cornerstone of a service economy) and a return to a more **balanced** U.S. larger economic model where the manufacturing and production base can be re-established *and competitive* based on American entrepreneurship and innovation.

The key words in the prior statement are "dependence" and "balanced". When a nation has an industrial manufacturing balance within the GDP there is far less dependence on the economic activity in global markets. In essence the U.S. can sustain itself, absorb global economic fluctuations and expand itself or contract itself depending on the free market.

When there is no balance, there is no longer a free market. The free market is sacrificed in favor of dependency, whether it's foreign oil or foreign manufacturing, the dependency outcome is essentially the same. Without balance there is an inherent loss of economic independence, and a consequential increase in economic risk.

No other economy in the world innovates like the U.S.A. Donald Trump sees this as a key advantage across all industry – including manufacturing and technology.

The benefit of cheap overseas labor, which is considered a global market disadvantage for the U.S., is offset by utilizing innovation and energy independence.

The third highest variable cost of goods beyond raw materials first, labor second, is energy. If the U.S. energy sector is unleashed -and fully developed- the manufacturing price of any given product will allow for global trade competition even with higher U.S. wage prices.

In addition the U.S. has a key strategic advantage with raw manufacturing materials such as: iron ore, coal, steel, precious metals and vast mineral assets which are needed in most new modern era manufacturing. Trump proposes we stop selling these valuable national assets to countries we compete against – they belong to the American people, they should be used for the benefit of American citizens. Period.

EXAMPLE: Currently China buys and recycles our heavy (steel) and light (aluminum) metal products (for pennies on the original manufacturing dollar) and then uses those metals to reproduce manufactured goods for sale back to the U.S. – Donald Trump is proposing we do the manufacturing ourselves with the utilization of our own resources; and we use the leverage from *any sales of these raw materials* in our international trade agreements.

When you combine FULL resource development (in a modern era) with with the removal of over-burdensome regulatory and compliance systems, necessarily filled with enormous bureaucratic costs, Donald Trump proposes we can lower the cost of production and be globally competitive. In essence, Trump changes the economic paradigm, and we no longer become a dependent nation relying on a service driven economy.

The cornerstone to the success of this economic turnaround is the keen capability of the U.S. worker to innovate on their own platforms. Americans, more than any country in the world, just know how to get things accomplished. Independence and self-sufficiency is part of the DNA of the larger American workforce.

In addition, an unquantifiable benefit comes from investment, where the smart money play -to get increased return on investment- becomes putting capital INTO the U.S. economy, instead of purchasing foreign stocks.

With all of the above opportunities in mind, this is how we get on the pathway to rebuilding our national infrastructure. The demand for labor increases, and as a consequence so too does the U.S. wage rate which has been stagnant (or non-existent) for the past three decades.

As the wage rate increases, and as the economy expands, the governmental dependency model is reshaped and simultaneously receipts to the U.S. treasury improve.

More money into the U.S Treasury and less dependence on welfare/social service programs have a combined exponential impact. You gain a dollar, and have no need to spend a dollar – the saved sum is doubled. That is how the SSI and safety net programs are saved under President Trump.

When you elevate your economic thinking you begin to see that all of the "entitlements" or expenditures become more affordable with an economy that is fully functional.

As the GDP of the U.S. expands, so does our ability to meet the growing need of the retiring U.S. worker. We stop thinking about how to best divide a limited economic pie, and begin thinking about how many more economic pies we can create.

Simply put, we begin to....

...Make America Great Again!

Authors note *as shared in 2016: If I absolutely did not believe this economic model was doable, I would never expand the concept and*

place advocacy upon it. I am an absolute believer that we can, as a nation, reignite a solid manufacturing base and generate an expanding middle class.

Yes, in the short term durable goods **may** *cost more, that's to be expected. However, these are durable goods, not disposable goods. As consumers we may have to spend a little more on maintenance and repair to offset an increase in durable goods, but that's a small price to pay to make the U.S. manufacturing base great again."* - H/T Sundance.

The Cultural Roots of Trumpism

By Geoffrey P. Hunt
January 23, 2018

"President Donald Trump's occasional unfiltered coarse cloudbursts belie a man who is enormously joyful, having an abundance of entertaining good humor easily expressed, fairly shared. Trump is having a ball, for good reasons.

Trump's first year as president may have been the most extraordinary since the 1840s. While Trump has disrupted almost all presidential governance and communication norms, his tenure so far has produced capital market gains of some $7 trillion, spreading investment wealth to millions of regular Joes and Marys, while tax cuts have already distributed $3 billion in bonuses and wage hikes to over 2 million workers and counting.

The Trump-inspired American economic revival, accompanied by a cultural earthquake in newfound respect, self-esteem, and optimism for working-class citizens, rural and urban – ignored and maligned since the industrial heartland was eviscerated in the 1980s – matches the economic and territorial expansions under presidents John Tyler and James Polk.

Westward expansion, Manifest Destiny, abetted by industrial innovation from the telegraph to steam engines to sewing machines, ushered in the longest economic growth period in American history – 1841 to 1859.

The 1840s also propelled the American Renaissance in literature and art. The fabulous Hudson River School of landscape painting, originating around 1825, spawned two major shifts in the 1840s:

landscapes capturing Easterners' imagination about the West and illustrations of people in everyday scenes with the Americana backdrops. Perhaps the best practitioner of the new genre was George Caleb Bingham, portrait painter and politician, who lived most of his life in Missouri.

Bingham captured the heart of the American spirit – a mix of personal liberty and economic fortunes – in his iconic 1846 painting, "The Jolly Flatboatmen," now owned by and usually on display at the National Gallery of Art.

NGA director Rusty Powell says The Jolly Flatboatmen is " the most important genre painting in American history."

No one knows whether Bingham's boatmen, dancing and luxuriating on the deck of a river flatboat barge loaded with furs, bolts of cloth, and other premium cargo, are floating downstream on the upper Missouri or Mississippi. The exact topography doesn't matter; the image conveying understated exuberance is infectious.

The solitary fiddler, the frying pan-tambourine man, and the other boatmen could have been figures drawn by Caravaggio, inviting the viewer to join in the moment, to take a seat on the hand-hewn oar or on top of the chicken coop – no more, no less.

Bingham's clarity of purpose matches his clarity of brushstrokes. The viewer's angle could be from a small river skiff, such as a Mackinaw boat. The closest boatman bemused at our attention seems contented enough, despite his toes sticking out from the welt of his shoe. The slightly impish man in the Quaker wide-awake hat, alongside the steering-oarsman, looks self-satisfied, confident, and prosperous enough.

Franklin Kelly, curator at the NGA, said this about "The Jolly Flatboatmen":

> It's very democratic. These are working people; they're wearing their ordinary clothes – tattered – but they're having a good time. It's that notion of a democratic art in a democratic society.

Donald Trump, the NYC luxury high rise-builder, should be the most unlikely populist egalitarian. Yet Trump would be at home with the jolly flatboatmen. These are the people who built the nation, unmolested by a suffocating federal government. By 1846, only Missouri and Iowa among the Missouri River territories had been admitted to the Union.

People of the frontier, anyplace west of the Appalachians, in the 1840s were tamers of the wilderness. Life could be nasty, brutish, and short, as wrote Hobbes in another century. Yet endurance, calculated risk-taking, commercial cleverness, and even desperation produced American pragmatism, and exeptionalism.

These are Hillary Clinton's deplorables. These are the Walmart shoppers. These are the truck-drivers, machine tool-operators, steamfitters, and grocery aisle shelf-stockers. These are the diverse line-up of Trump voters in Youngstown, Ohio, who stunned CNN about a week ago with their full-throated approval of Trump's first year.

Bingham, the painter, was no stranger to the imperfect, messy features of frontier and small-town democracy. He dabbled in politics as a Missouri state senator and Missouri treasurer, among other statewide offices.

In his "The County Election" (St. Louis Museum of Art), Bingham displays both porcelain and pockmarks on the faces of a remarkable collection of backgrounds and temperaments, where each vote is equal, the outcome accepted.

There are four sweeping themes occupying American socio-economic history: westward expansion, slavery, immigration, and industrialization. These themes have a common narrative: labor and natural resources. The narrative about labor invokes contradictory notions about liberty and submission. Moreover, the history of the American people is a complex saga of bloodshed for freedom from authoritarian tyranny, repudiation of an aristocracy to assure equality of opportunity, and the yearning for self-sufficiency and dignity.

The delivery of socio-economic justice, ameliorating the worst excesses within the labor narrative, has always been through the gifts of fertile land, "the fruited plain," an abundance of natural resources. The "peoples' history," expropriated by deconstructive historians using disingenuous storylines of labor oppression and subjugation, is really about rivers, harbors, timber, cotton, corn, wheat, coal, oil, and iron ore. Ships, sails, barges, mills, machines, furnaces, coke and coal, iron, steel, rails and roads, steam engines, trucks, tractors, and airplanes – this is the stuff of nation-building, prosperity, and empire – and ultimate redemption.

Donald Trump gets it. There are no Democrats remaining who get it. No one should underestimate Trump's legion of Jolly Flatboatmen who freely voted for their self-interest and can now dance to their own tune, all because of Donald Trump "

-H/T Geoffrey P. Hunt

https://www.americanthinker.com/articles/2018/01/the_cultural_root s_of_trumpism.html#ixzz5d64lYf00
Published with permission from the American Thinker.

President Trump's SOTU Affirmed Liberty
to Unresponsive Subversives

By E. Jeffrey Ludwig
February 8, 2019

"An hour before Pres. Donald Trump's State of the Union Address, I opened my mail. It included a thank-you note regarding a contribution I had made to a right-wing organization. The author of the note quoted Nikita Khrushchev, who said, "You Americans are so gullible. No, you won't accept communism outright, but we'll keep feeding you small doses of socialism until you finally wake up and find you already have communism." The author of the thank-you note was revolted by this remark by N.K. and knew I would be as well.

I grew up during the Cold War and understood that communism was not merely an alternative theory of politics and economics to that held by most Americans, but was a living and breathing threat to our freedom emanating 24-7 from the USSR, the PRC, and a determined fifth column of traitorous leftists living in these United States. Our conflict with communism was not a mere academic or drawing room debate between gentleman-scholars. Rather, the ardent supporters of communism wished to extract the essence of our freedom and opportunities from our society.

In the name of curbing the rich, they wish to curb us all, grab power, assert governmental force over every area of our lives, and make themselves arbiters of every life decision we make – where we live, what kind of work each of us does, where and when we can and cannot travel, how to heat our homes or even build our homes, where to go to school, how many children to have, how long we live and under what conditions we live, and even the thoughts we think. Almost all that we now consider "private" they would refashion and reconfigure to be seen as "public." Our individual rights would be subsumed under collective rights.

As Richard Overy relates in his remarkable volume, *The Dictators: Hitler's Germany, Stalin's Russia*, under the Soviet Union system of law, a person could be deemed guilty of a crime simply because he was documented to have had *thoughts* similar to the thoughts of those who actually plotted and committed a crime even if he had had no part in planning or carrying out the crime. Thus, when I see Bernie Sanders's bespectacled face, I see not just another person with whom I have some differences of opinion, but, behind his college professor visage, a hideous expression of hatred for all that we hold dear. In like manner do I perceive the other leftists of the Democratic Party with their pro-communism agenda despite their attempts to present those views as mainstream or make them sound less threatening by calling them socialistic.

Pres. Donald Trump spat in the face of the socialists and socialists in sheep's clothing of the Democratic Party during Tuesday evening's State of the Union address. "America was founded on liberty and independence and not government coercion, domination, and control," he said to Republican applause. He continued, "We are born free and we will stay free. **Tonight, we renew our resolve that America will never be a socialist country.**" These sentences cleared the air. There is no hiding from the truth encapsulated in these words. Fresh air blew through the hall and could be felt over the airwaves.

The Democrats should be repudiating the extreme leftists in their party; instead, they are embracing the far left ideology. During the 1930s and 1940s, the Democrats went through a crisis where they had to repudiate the extreme left wing of the party, which roughly can be designated as those led by Henry Wallace. President Harry Truman fired Wallace from his position as secretary of commerce because he perceived Wallace as being too conciliatory toward the Soviet Union. Wallace subsequently formed the Progressive Party and ran for president against Truman and the Republican candidate, Thomas Dewey, in 1948 but garnered only 2.4% of the vote. Here was a case where the Democratic Party's leader repudiated the far-left wing of that party. Nevertheless, it was an ironic and striking reality that a large percentage of the Socialist Party platform of 1912 had been implemented in the U.S., including the graduated income tax, by the time Wallace was rejected. Most of the implementation came during the New Deal under President Franklin D. Roosevelt. Only in their program of "Collective Ownership" were the goals of the Socialist Party not met over time. The people of the U.S. decided on regulation instead of ownership. The socialists wanted ownership of all banks, all transportation, all mines, all means of communication, and all land.

Similar trends can be seen in the labor movement in the 1940s era. Many unions that had been strongly supportive of Pres. Franklin Roosevelt because of his initiative in getting the Wagner Act through Congress at the same time tried to purge their ranks of communist leadership. My own father was a union activist with the Transport Workers' Union. That union had been formed both by men who were communist unionists and by non-communist unionists. Under the leadership of Michael Quill, whose base was staunchly Irish Catholic and still held many so-called "bourgeois values," repudiated and kicked out the communist wing of the union, also in 1948, as the Cold War picked up a head of steam.

Earlier in the century, Eugene V. Debs had run for president three times as leader of the Socialist Party, but his aggressive objection to World War I led to his imprisonment and severely set back the socialist-communist agenda in the U.S.

Make no mistake about it: the Socialist Party was adamantly against private ownership of property. One need only read its platform of 1912 to see that. Labeling themselves socialists to distinguish themselves from communists should be taken with a grain of salt. Early on, the socialists realized that the word "communism" had so many negative connotations for Americans that the term "socialism" would be more palatable to the citizenry. However, their desire to control (not merely regulate) all major industries was explicit, with control of smaller industries and businesses implied.

By the last presidential election of 2016, the platform of the socialists had morphed into 248 bullet points, a veritable stew of negativism that advocated for intense federal controls to invade almost every area of American life. Today's Democrats are no longer repudiating communist ideas and ideals, but are embracing in ever greater numbers its calls for universal Medicare, universal free higher education, open borders under the rubric of compassion, elimination of the electoral college, and an embrace of worldwide climate change agendas with a massive redistribution of wealth to the Third World and ever increasing government controls over every detail of daily life. These policy themes that would require a tremendous curtailment of freedom are being embraced and advocated by Democrats rather than repudiated.

The communist focus of 1948 was repudiated by the Democrats of 1948, but it is being incorporated as the mainstream ideas and ideals of that party today, and individual choice and individual property rights are disparaged. During the State Modern liberalism Modern liberalism of the Union address, President Trump spoke forcefully and directly into the faces of subversion. Although many on the left were dressed in white, they represented the dark side of humanity. All the purity was in Trump's liberty-loving remarks."

-H/T E.Jeffrey Ludwig

https://www.americanthinker.com/articles/2019/02/president_trump s_sotu_address_affirmed_liberty_to_unresponsive_subversives.html_
Published with permission from the American Thinker

The Exceptional Trump

By Michael Widlanski
July 17, 2019

"Donald Trump, unlike Barack Obama & Company, loves talking about America's "exceptional" qualities, but we tend to overlook the importance of the exceptional qualities of Trump himself.

No, this will not be a suck-up exercise about the current occupant of 1600 Pennsylvania Avenue.

A serious discussion of President Trump and his record should not neglect Trump's faults and mistakes, but it must honestly assess how Trump's own background has shaped events in America and the world.

In many respects, Trump is a fulfilment of the vision of America by the French historian Alexis De Tocqueville, who studied and described American exceptionalism almost 200 years ago, and his words are still accurate.

De Tocqueville saw what made America special, different from Europe, and one of his observations was that great men in America tended to go into "commerce" (today we would say business), leaving politics for more mediocre people.

If one looks at Congress, one finds a collection of mostly mediocrities, failed lawyers and future lobbyists, rarely anyone who has proven himself or herself in any field like business, science or medicine. This is especially true of the Democrats, though there are always some Republican mediocrities, too.

One is hard-pressed to find a Democrat in the House or Senate from New York, California or Illinois who ran a successful business like Donald Trump, George W. Bush or Carly Fiorina, had a medical career like

Ben Carson John Barraso or Rand Paul, or led the Screen Actors Guild like Ronald Reagan.

Being an independent businessman who becomes a presidential candidate — whether Donald Trump or H. Ross Perot (who died this month) — promotes independent thought, and it exposes the candidate to creative concepts that are out-of-the-box and out-of-Washington.

Trump's critics emphasize Trump's Twitter eruptions (and they are sometimes right to criticize), but they minimize the fact that Trump does NOT have the habits of the play-it-safe politician but rather more of the can-do man of commerce, constantly looking for ways to solve problems and curb inefficiencies.

Even before he actually took office, Trump was trying to cut deals and cut costs — whether revising plans for the new Air Force One or bringing more jobs back to Ohio and Michigan. His work routine — long hours and personal involvement — showed he would spend less time golfing in Hawaii and vacationing in Camp David.

Any fair assessment of Trump starts by realizing that Trump knows how to work, how to make others work for him, how to make money and how to make money work for you.

Donald Trump is the first modern president who has learned life's lessons of how economic forces work. Trump does not need to read Paul Samuelson or (God Forbid) Paul Krugman. He understands how to leverage money for building a hotel in New York (that others said would never be built) or how to leverage money, tariffs and sanctions to deter, seduce and coerce China, Iran and Russia, and even Mexico and Canada.

This is a businessman who loves to take credit and hates to walk away from a fight but who loves it even more when he makes a deal no one else could make, collecting the profits (even without taking credit).

You will not hear the "experts" at NBC or CNN or NYT or WashPost admit this, but this exceptional man, who wanted to deal with Vladimir Putin, was also the first US president whose forces actually fired at the Russians — twice in Syria. Tell that to the huffy puffy hallucinators who claim Trump "colluded with Russia."

These are the same partisan geniuses who insist Barack Obama deserved a Nobel Peace Prize, ignoring Obama's hand in bringing more destruction to Syria, millions of refugees to Europe, a failed state in Libya, and nuclear bombs within the grasp of the Iranian ayatollahs.

Trump's foreign policy record is an amazing reversal of Obama's failures, and Trump's economic record is real.

They are exceptional achievements, especially extraordinary for being achieved in the teeth of the "resistance" deployed against him by the media-Democrat team.

One need not be a Trump devotee to appreciate the amazing record of more jobs and higher wages achieved — despite the forecasts by "experts." One need not be a fan of Trump's to appreciate that his attention to Asian affairs was not the kind of policy fiction of Obama-Clinton-Kerry

By all means, keep criticizing Trump — his rhetoric, his style, his long ties, his hair, ya-da-ya-da, but step back to appreciate the full picture.

Take exception to elements of Trump's style, but not Trump's exceptionalism.

Dr. Michael Widlanski taught political communication for two decades at The Hebrew University, Bar Ilan University and as a visiting professor at Washington University in St. Louis in 2007-8 and at the University of California, Irvine in 2014. Earlier he was a reporter at The New York Times, Cox Newspapers, Israeli Army Radio and Israel Television. "

-H/T Michael Widlansky

https://www.americanthinker.com/articles/2019/07/the_exceptional_trump.html
Published with permission from the American Thinker.

Trump and the Character Question

By Brian Joondeph
January 7, 2019

"At the midpoint of Donald Trump's presidency, those in his party who seemingly should be supporting him are as critical as ever. Now it's the issue of his character.

NeverTrump Jonah Goldberg recently penned an article, "Character is Destiny," proclaiming that "Trump's character will be his downfall."

Evidence of this poor character is "[t]he president's style, specifically his insults and Twitter addiction." Goldberg goes farther, saying, "They are the product of astonishing levels of narcissism, insecurity, and intellectual incuriosity."

He cites examples of how Trump fires Cabinet members or other officials, not face to face to face, but through surrogates, and his "[p]raise for dictators and insults for allies, his need to create new controversies to eclipse old ones, and his inexhaustible capacity to lie and fabricate history."

Let's start unpacking this.

Tweets? It's Trump's way of bypassing a hostile media establishment. Looking at Twitter at the time of this writing, the Trump hostility is obvious. I see one tweet from CNN: "Former President Barack Obama lists his favorite books, songs and movies of 2018."

And another tweet from CNN: "Trump's lies sometimes seem strategic. But polls show that most Americans see right through it & realize he's untrustworthy." Could the contrasting messages be more different?

Is it a Twitter addiction or the only way he can get his message out, running the gauntlet of constant adversarial and negative media coverage?

CEOs delegate authority and responsibility. It's not at all unusual for the CEO not to personally deliver the pink slip, and typically, by the time it happens, it's no surprise to the person being let go. Big deal.

Praise for dictators? I'm reminded of the old saying that you catch more flies with honey than with vinegar. These foreign leaders, whether Vladimir Putin or Kim Jung-un, have huge egos. What good does insulting them on the world stage do to further negotiations? A better strategy is to be nice to them publicly to let them save face at home while getting tough behind closed doors. Common sense. Look at the results rather than the appearance.

Insults for allies? Like NATO allies needing to be shamed into paying their fair share, a term the left loves, for NATO, honoring their agreements? Past presidents have raised the issue and let it go. Trump is calling them on it. Or challenging Angela Merkel on her side deal for natural gas with Russia, in violation of NATO. It's called accountability.

Trump's history of womanizing as a character flaw? Sure, but that blanket covers many past presidents. At least for Trump, it was decades ago, not while he was president, something that cannot be said for many Oval Office occupants.

Let's look at an organization famous for building character, at least until the social justice termites chewed it up: the Boy Scouts. Their mission is simple: "The BSA's goal is to train youth in responsible citizenship, character development, and self-reliance."

How would President Trump's character measure up as a Boy Scout based on the Scout Law? Here are a few examples.

Trustworthy. Trump is following through on his campaign promises: constitutionalist judges, tax cuts, better trade deals, getting our military out of foreign entanglements, trying (in the face of Congressional opposition) to secure the border.

Loyal. Trump is loyal to his supporters and those loyal to him. He gave General Mattis, fired previously by Obama, a second chance and stuck with him for two years despite significant differences of opinion.

Helpful. Trump regularly visits disaster areas, whether a shooting, a wildfire, or a hurricane. Some might call it a photo op, but he is there to assure local officials of federal support and assistance.

Friendly. The media complain about accessibility. But has a president ever been more willing to stop on his way to Marine One to chat with the press? Sometimes he will spend 20-30 minutes, answering whatever questions they have.

Courteous. Trump respects the White House and the office of the presidency. He is rarely seen in public out of his suit and tie – unlike a predecessor who frequented the Oval Office in sweaty running gear.

Cheerful. Despite overwhelming opposition from all quarters, even from many within his own party, Trump remains upbeat and optimistic. He maintains a cheerfulness that few mortals could achieve under the weight of constant criticism and hostility. Just look at any of his campaign rallies for his cheer and optimism.

Thrifty. Trump, unlike the rest of Washington, D.C., realizes that our national debt is equal to America's yearly economic output and is growing year by year. He has forgone his own presidential salary and is trimming the fat within the executive branch as much as possible – and urging Congress, albeit unsuccessfully, to do the same.

Brave. Trump is no coward. He is currently playing chicken with Pelosi and Schumer in the government shutdown, as well as with a host of foreign leaders, both friend and foe, getting the best for America.

Clean. The current White House is free of rapper thugs, randy interns, race-hustlers, and other riffraff who frequented previous administrations on a regular basis.

Reverent. It is impossible to know a man's heart, but Trump appears to have grown into his faith over the past several years, quietly and without virtue-signaling – unlike some of his predecessors, who used bibles and church attendance as props or photo opportunities.

By Boy Scout criteria, President Trump is certainly of good character. Is he flawed, as we all are in our own ways? Of course, but such is human nature.

Regardless, Trump was elected by the people, character and all. He set out a clear agenda for America, attempting to reverse decades of mismanagement, foreign and domestic, pulling the country back from the brink of "radical transformation" into something most Americans don't want.

It's a testament to his strength of character that he is able to persevere, advancing his agenda, despite opposition from so many quarters. Lesser men would fold to the establishment, seeking compromise with the uni-party and accolades from the media for doing so.

Abraham Lincoln once said, "Character is like a tree and reputation like a shadow. The shadow is what we think of it; the tree is the real thing." In Trump's case, the tree is what he is doing and accomplishing. The shadow is everything else – the tweets and "character" that the NeverTrumps are in a lather over.

As the sun goes down, so do the shadows. But the tree remains. Critics such as Mitt Romney would be far wiser focusing on the tree rather than the shadows."

-H/T Brian C Joondeph, M.D., MPS
is a Denver-based physician and writer.

https://www.americanthinker.com/articles/2019/01/trump_and_the_
character_question.html#ixzz5c5gS75Xu
Published with permission from the American Thinker.

The rare wisdom of our president is a gift

By Don Sucher
March 24, 2019

"Politicians are used to seeing cowardice and being cowards. So used to it are they that they cannot even imagine there being another way.

Our president has proven to be quite different. He is fearless. He is bold. He acts. He accomplishes. (What he would be accomplishing if those in his party had the courage to support him is hard to conceive.) If one takes a moment to look at his brilliance, it is a truly rare and beautiful thing.

First off, the attacks were made to wear him down and wear him out. To make him sue (and compromise) for peace. He did not.

Two, they thought they could make him overreact, go beyond his jurisdiction. He did not do that, either.

Three, when attacks on him directly failed, they went after his family. The media in the end were saying his children were going to be indicted. He did not wince. (Neither did they.)

And what is even more an indicator of genius is that often the very thing that drove his enemies mad — and made it obvious to onlookers that they *were* mad (and thus not be believed) was seen by his supporters in a positive light. His good humor, for instance.

This is a rare form of leadership — temperance crossed with almost outlandish boldness. (How often can those two words describe the same man at the very same time?) Thank God, it is rarely needed.

That the "wise" cannot see this is to be expected. They worship what they themselves are: wordy, hapless, false, and ineffective.

Our president is none of these things. He is truly something else.

Something rare. Something wonderful.

To think this nation received such a leader at this critical time by mere chance is to this writer unimaginable."

-H/T Don Sucher

https://www.americanthinker.com/blog/2019/03/the_rare_wisdom_o f_our_president_is_a_gift.html#ixzz5j6nufn9z

Published with permission from the American Thinker.

What Trump does not do...and it's fantastic

By Majid Mohammadi
March 16, 2019

"When Democrats lost to a non-politician in 2016, they could not swallow the failure and began to degrade their opponent's victory (by manufacturing "Russia collusion"), insult people who voted for the winner (calling them racist), and assassinate the character of the winner (calling him a dictator). To make the case for the third act, they invented a story that Donald Trump likes dictators and wants to be one and will not leave office if not elected in 2020. But his actions show the opposite. Trump does not want to be a king or a dictator, while his predecessors behaved as if they wanted to be.

To demonstrate this fact, I will provide examples of what Trump has not done and what King Barack H. Obama and King George W. Bush did. Here is a list:

1. Trump does not invite singers and performers to the White House to sing and perform for him and his family, while Obama and Bush did. They sat like kings and used our tax money to be entertained.

2. Trump does not go to Kennedy Center honors or Mark Twain prize ceremonies to sit in a special place and be watched by the crowd as a king.

3. Trump does not perform at the White House Correspondents' dinner as the chief of the country. He does not care about entertaining the media and being praised by them.

4. Trump calls media as they are (biased and unprofessional)

without violating their rights. He does not need them to praise him as King Obama and King Bush did. All dictators love to be praised. Trump does not care about the elite's expectations.

5. Trump is focused on results and delivering his promises. He does not keep people in office who do not deliver.

6. Against all leftists' propaganda, Trump has not gained any personal benefit from being in power. All reports show that his business is not as good as before 2016.

7. Trump did not bow to the king of Saudi Arabia as Obama did. He did not praise Putin as Bush did. He did not try to normalize a relationship with Cuban dictators and did not write personal nice letters to the dictator of Iran, as Obama did.

8. Trump is not writing fat checks to people who chant "death to America" (like Hamas).

9. Trump did not need any praise from Europeans and pushed them to pay their fair share in NATO.

10. Trump did not budge to socialists, Islamists, and fascists, while both Obama and Bush were lenient toward them. Their failures were effective in giving a boost to those groups.

The reasons Trump does not do these things are less important than the not doing them itself. Trump, whatever he is, is the elected leader of American people and has behaved as an elected leader.

Nobody is perfect. Democratically elected leaders are supposed to be average — average government by average people. Our founding fathers never wanted (fake) philosopher-kings as our leaders."

-H/T Majid Mohammadi

Trump: Our Lincoln?

By Randolph Parrish
January 30, 2019

"In 1861, President Lincoln confronted a section of the body politic that refused to accept his election. Instead of hunkering down and resorting to the ballot the next time around, they simply repudiated the entire electoral process and voted (with their feet and arms) for negation of the election results. Lincoln responded on July 4:

> "Our popular government has often been called an experiment. Two points in it our people have already settled – the successful establishing and the successful administering of it.
>
> "One still remains – its successful maintenance against a formidable internal attempt to overthrow it.

"It is now for them to demonstrate to the world that those who can fairly carry an election can also suppress a rebellion; that ballots are the rightful and peaceful successors of bullets; and that when ballots have fairly and constitutionally decided, there can be no successful appeal back to bullets; that there can no be no successful appeal except to ballots themselves, at succeeding elections.

"Such will be a great lesson of peace; teaching men that what they cannot take by an election neither can they take by a war; teaching all the folly of being the beginners of a war."

–July 4, 1861: Address to Congress

No president since Lincoln has faced the prospect of an internal rebellion as has Trump. The departments of his own government are aligned against him. The Justice Department in no way answers his summons. The FBI uses overwhelming force to intimidate his supporters. The intelligence agencies conspire for his removal. The media, some of which appear to be merely part of the same apparatus, lie to the public in order to foment hysteria and create a popular clamor.

"... a monstrous usurpation, a criminal wrong, and an act of national suicide."

–The Chicago Times, on the
Emancipation Proclamation

What is at stake, as in Lincoln's day, is not merely who is the occupant of the White House. It is the survival of our democracy itself.

The people voted for Trump in 2016. Immediately, calls were heard for the Electoral College to be unfaithful to the electorate and select someone other than the winner. There were cries that votes had been stolen (though the factual totals indicate that more fraudulent votes were cast for the opposition than for Trump).

There were efforts to get the Cabinet to invoke the 25th Amendment. Trump, like Lincoln, was lambasted as an incompetent who lowered the standards of the presidency by using tweets.

> "His weak, wishy-washy, namby-pamby efforts, imbecile in matter, disgusting in manner, have made us the laughing stock of the whole world. The European powers will despise us because we have no better material out of which to make a President[.] ... Take him from his vocation and he loses even these small characteristics and indulges in simple twaddle which would disgrace a well bred school boy."
>
> –Salem Advocate, 1861

Like Lincoln, Trump was temperamentally unfit:

> "He is evidently a person of very inferior cast of character, wholly unequal to the crisis."
>
> –Edward Everett in his diary

The reason for Trump's impeachment doesn't matter. If he hadn't committed treason (based on a phony dossier – shades of the Dreyfus case and its phony *bordereau)*, then he was guilty of accepting unlawful emoluments while in office (because people stayed at his hotels).

Only the end result counted – that a duly elected president, chosen by the people, should not be allowed to hold office because one faction refused to accept the electoral result and was determined to replace him with a man (or woman) of its own choosing.

What's at stake in possible impeachment hearings, as well as the Mueller investigation, is no less than it was in Lincoln's day: do the people have the right to select their own government, or are their votes to count for nothing, and a faction, a gang, a cabal, or whatever name is given to it, be allowed a veto over the electorate to protect its own interests and purposes?

We are in a struggle no less significant than the Civil War, and testing the same principles, but the prize is worth the fight, if we can endure:

> "[Once this is accomplished, America's] form of government is saved to the world; its beloved history, and cherished memories are vindicated; and its future fully assured, and rendered inconceivably grand. To you, more than to any others, the privilege if given, to assure that happiness, and swell that grandeur, and to link your names therewith foever.
>
> -Appeal to the Border States"

-H/T Randolph Parrish

http://www.americanthinker.com/blog/2019/01/trump_our_lincoln.html

Published with permission from the American Thinker.

Townhall *Daily*

Donald Trump: America's Winston Churchill?

William Marshall
Posted: Mar 28, 2019 10:29 AM

The opinions expressed by columnists are their own and do not represent the views of Townhall.com.

Source: AP Photo/Evan Vucci

"Our times resemble nothing if not 1930s Britain. Our politics are roiled by tensions between a large (largely young), ignorant population of idealists taken in with the concept of socialism/communism and an older, wiser populace who recognize the greatness of the contributions of our country. We face external enemies today as ruthless as those faced by England in the '30s. Our alliances are complex and our national fiscal situation is deeply concerning, just as the UK's was. The similarities between Britain of that era and America of today, to my mind, are almost eerie. And the similarities between Donald Trump and Winston Churchill bear description.

I've taken comfort in these troubled times, however, in reading William Manchester's three-volume biography of Winston Churchill, *The Last Lion.* In the midst of Britain's turmoil in the early 20th century was an unusual man. Really, an incredible man. Winston Churchill. He was pugnacious beyond belief, maddening to his enemies, and often to his friends as well. Sound familiar?

The source of his inability to "fit in" was his own brilliance. And like most brilliant people, he recognized the disparity between his own immense intellectual powers and those of the lesser lights with whom he had to interact, producing a tiresome sense of pushing a Sisyphean boulder up a hill. In the governance of the British Empire, with its multitude of responsibilities, this was no mean feat. This intellectual imbalance naturally made for contentious relationships.

And like other genius statesmen in parlous times, such as Abraham Lincoln, Churchill was beset by the "Black Dog" - his euphemism for what we might call depression. One way that he coped with it was through self-medication with alcohol. Another way he coped was by directing his prodigious energies and powerful intellect into his unrivalled command of the English language and his preternatural understanding of history and England's role in it.

And speaking of Churchill's copious use of alcohol, I'm reminded of another interesting parallel with Trump. Although President Trump is a teetotaler, he shares with Churchill a mastery of the put-down. Churchill was once allegedly rebuked by his perpetual nemesis, Lady Astor, who accused Churchill of being "disgustingly drunk." Without missing a beat, Churchill responded, "My dear, you are ugly, and what's more, you are disgustingly ugly. But tomorrow I shall be sober and you will still be disgustingly ugly."

Ouch! Touché.

Is that really much different from Megyn Kelly starting a question to Trump in a 2016 GOP debate with: "You've called women you don't like 'fat pigs, dogs, slobs, and disgusting animals,'" and Trump abruptly cutting in with: "Only Rosie O'Donnell."

Burn.

Not quite as artful as Churchill, maybe, but equally devastating - and maybe not wholly undeserved, given O'Donnell's treatment of Trump over the years.

Moving along, Churchill's love for Victorian English ideals reflected his belief in the greatness of British culture and bears considerable resemblance to the visceral love that Donald Trump feels for America — or the American Ideal. In another time, that might have been referred to as Manifest Destiny. The sense that God foreordained America to be the vessel through which He expanded human greatness and individual dignity, in opposition to some ever-present urge among many people to collectivize, to oppress, to assert dominance in the view that they alone possess the knowledge to achieve human happiness through the imposition of will.

For Churchill, this evil imposition of will took a very clear form in Adolph Hitler. As Manchester describes in his epic biography, genius is not some great cognitive ability to unravel mysteries that stump others (although there may be an element of that). Rather, it is the ability to see some vitally important goal in the distance and direct oneself toward that goal relentlessly, despite all the slings and arrows that one might encounter along the way. It is a resoluteness in one's drive to realize that vision. In the case of a great statesman like Churchill, that vision took the form of recognizing the great threat to liberty for Western civilization that Hitler represented.

Unlike Churchill, Trump did not spend his life immersed in politics. President Trump arguably had a much more rounded life. He created a company that built great architectural projects and a brand that represented perfection. That is not to detract at all from the contributions of Churchill, whose great collection of literary works dwarf almost any other from the 20th century. It is only to point out the wildly divergent paths these two political giants took to come to a very similar place: an internalized belief in the greatness of Western civilization and the importance of ensuring its continued survival.

Several years ago, on the eve of President Trump's election, I wrote about my sense that Donald Trump possessed the best and worst qualities of what I called a "junkyard dog." I was trying to refine a metaphor that others had been using for him as a bull in a china shop, which I felt missed the mark. Trump was not a blunderbuss, as his critics would have it, smashing delicate, highly refined policies and alliances through arrogance, ignorance and gratuitous hostility. Rather, he possessed an intense, internalized understanding of American Exceptionalism, so obviously absent in our previous president, and sought to restore that exceptionalism through a combination of force of will and a lifetime of unparalleled deal-making expertise. He possessed the qualities of a highly protective guard dog who was fiercely defensive of his property (our country) and his master (the American people), and would sacrifice his life, if necessary, in that pursuit.

My conviction as expressed in that earlier essay has only increased, as I've watched President Trump endure an unprecedented onslaught from a Deep State comprised of Democrats, Never Trumpers and entrenched government apparatchiks, as well as 90 percent of the mainstream media, virtually all of Hollywood and academia from coast to coast.

While Donald Trump may not have possessed a deep grounding in conservative philosophy before his ascent to the presidency, he's demonstrated that he possessed something far more important: a love for America as its Founders envisioned it.

In the same way, Winston Churchill understood how the British Empire lifted so much of the world out of darkness and into a better, more civilized place - with education and healthcare provided for the poor, markets for the industrious to sell their wares and thereby raise their station in life, and administrative and legal structures to provide due process and equal protection under the law.

I, for one, feel reassured that we have the equivalent of the British Bulldog sitting in the White House. Let us hope that President Trump has as successful a tenure as head of state as did Winston. He seems well on his way."

–H/T William Marshall

https://townhalldaily.com/article/america's_winston_churchill
H/T to Townhall.com

What do Washington, Churchill, and Trump have in common?

By Caroline Rausch
May 29, 2019

"Winston Churchill appears to have had an uncanny prescience of his own destiny. While still at Harrow, in a conversation with his contemporary Sir Murland Evans, Winston (then 16) remarked:

"I can see vast changes coming over a now peaceful world; great upheavals, terrible struggles, wars such as one cannot imagine. ... London will be attacked, and I will be very prominent in the defense of London."

Winston saw himself as a champion of democracy against tyranny and was profoundly aware of his own role and destiny. Indeed, he believed that God had placed him on Earth to carry out heroic deeds for the protection of Christian civilization and human progress.

Winston certainly was divinely protected. As a young officer, he took part in many battles, always rushing to the center of every conflict, fighting with fearless bravery and conspicuous valor, without regard for his personal safety, winning high commendation from his commanding officers and praise from his fellow subalterns. He participated in the last cavalry charge at Obdurman in the Sudan. All in a line, the horses of the 400 officers started slowly at a trot, gradually speeding up to a gallop, then plunging into a terrible collision. The 1,200 dervishes opposing them seemed to come up from the sand. Winston shot six or seven with his Mauser, one of whom lunged up at him with a spear. Although the fighting was fierce, Winston escaped death or injury, which was to be his lot his whole life long. When he was lord of the admiralty, he was on a ship struck by three German torpedoes, but they didn't explode. In

New York, he was rammed by a taxi — the impact would have killed anyone else, but he recovered after a time in a hospital. And once, while still young, he fell 30 yards down through some trees and was unconscious for three days, delaying his entrance to Sandhurst. While building a tree house for his children, he fell and dislocated his shoulder, and the dislocation kept coming and going his life long. He also crashed planes he was flying, but with only minor injuries. He lived to be 90.

Another such phenomenon was George Washington. There is an incredible account of Washington's preservation when he was an officer in the British army under General Braddock in the French and Indian Wars. His regiment was attacked by Indians using guerrilla tactics. Braddock was mortally wounded. There was enormous loss of life (75% of the officers and more than 700 troops) due to the incompetence and confusion of Braddock himself. Washington wrote about this incident in a letter to his brother as follows:

> I had four bullets through my coat, two horses were shot from under me, yet I escaped unhurt, though death was leveling my companions on every side around me.

Washington attributed this wonderful escape from even a wound to the overruling providence of God.

The Indians regarded the matter in the same light. About fifteen years after the battle, while surveying some lands near the mouth of the Great Kanawha River, Washington was visited by an old chief who told him he had been present at that battle, that he had singled him out and repeatedly fired his rifle at him, that he had ordered his young warriors to make him their only target, but that on finding all their bullets turned aside by some invisible and inscrutable interposition, he was convinced that the hero at whom he had so truly and often aimed must be, for some wise purpose, specially protected by the Great Spirit. He now came to testify his veneration.

Washington was six foot three inches in height and had broad shoulders. The Indians could not possibly have missed him.

I think Donald Trump can be added to these other two. In a YouTube video called "Trump Chosen By God," which has now been pulled, there was a prophecy that said Trump is divinely protected — nothing can harm him. Let the Secret Service continue to diligently guard him, but he stands under God's protecting wings and is doing God's work — not only for our Republic, but the light that shines from him is influencing the whole world. Everything that happened to him in his life so far, the successes and the failures, was preparation for his high calling. As he is a multi-millionaire, he could be relaxing in some beautiful, luxurious place, playing golf and enjoying the good life. That he has chosen to dedicate his life to serving us, taking all the slings and arrows hurled at him by the evil and the ignorant, the dreadful abuse, means he loves us, the American people, and we ought to love him in return. The majority of us do."

-H/T Caroline Rausch

https://www.americanthinker.com/blog/2019/05/what_do_washing-
ton_churchill_and_trump_have_in_common.html
Published with permission from the American Thinker.

Trump as Alexander the Great

By Bill Schanefelt
July 2, 2019

"It has been averred that "throughout his military career, Alexander won every battle that he personally commanded." Donald J. Trump, on the other hand, has made billions; lost and owed billions; made more billions; won the presidency against overwhelming odds; and has battled and is battling Democrats, the Establishment, and foreign powers on multiple fronts, with wins and losses.

A Fox commentator on evaluating Trump's gambit of a possible meeting with Kim at the DMZ said something along the lines of "it is the sign of a great leader that he is willing to risk a great loss in pursuit of a great gain." Had it not panned out in the actual meeting, it would have been an embarrassing loss for Trump. Fortunately for all, it did.

I am not an expert on Alexander, but I think it is safe to say Alexander risked defeat in many of his battles en route to his conquest of much of what was then the "known world," but he did win those battles and got far into the Subcontinent.

We'll eventually learn if Trump will cross his Indus, but Lordy, Lordy, the ride/war is great fun to watch as it's passing!

To the point, history might well conclude that the DMZ meeting was Trump's Gordian Knot moment. As legend holds, Alexander sliced the knot with his sword in order to be the one who would be destined "to become ruler of all of Asia." In the same way, Trump's stepping into North Korea might portend his solving of the multitude of hitherto intractable foreign and domestic problems with which he is now dealing.

Illustration by H.A. Guerber.

Might!

It was indeed a small step for a man, in Neil Armstrong's words, but we are yet a long way from learning if it was also a giant leap for mankind.

Trump "has done" with process. He has put process behind him and is confronting the issues in his own way — to hell with process (I'd love to use the expression I would use in Puerto Rico, but this is a family site).

Democrats, their judicial and media allies, entrenched bureaucrats, and NeverTrumps of all stripes will continue to fight him at every step, but he intends to pursue his goals to his last day.

Like Alexander, he will deceive, outmaneuver, and trick his enemies, but he intends to win by any legal means.

Iran is now his greatest challenge, and, unless the mullahs forestall his efforts by taking rash actions, watch for the unexpected there."

H/T Bill Schanefelt

H/T to Sundance for the inspiration behind and notions in this post.

The author is retired, his profile may be found on LinkedIn, and he usually responds to emails sent to bilschan@hotmail.com.

https://www.americanthinker.com/blog/2019/07/trump_as_alexander_the_great_.html
Published with permission from the American Thinker.

Does anyone doubt that Trump is the *Rocky* of American politics?

By Patricia McCarthy
June 19, 2019

"President Trump's rally on Tuesday to officially launch his 2020 campaign for re-election was a tour-de-force. The twenty thousand people in the arena, along with the thousands of people outside watching on jumbo screens were all on the same page: He has been a great President these past two and a half years and they want more of the same.

The crowd was excited, happy, and phenomenally supportive of the President, much to the chagrin of the angry left. And boy are they angry. They have lost any semblance of tolerance or open-mindedness. The radicalized American Left is now motivated by one thing, one thing only: destroy Trump. If they must obliterate the country as founded to do it, so be it. That is how deranged the Democrats in Congress and the anti-Trump moonbats — who spend their days in misery for nothing — actually are. There is no accounting for their anguish.

Trump has been a great President thus far. Is this perhaps why they are so mad? He has accomplished in two years what no president since Reagan did and done it in less time. This is what is called the psychopathic rage of envy. They are embarrassed by their own failure to transform the nation under the radar into their Alinskyite version of the Soviet Union. Like Hillary and the rest of the Left, they have always been thoroughly convinced that the bulk of the American people are sheep, or lemmings, easily led by their intellectual betters — them.

These self-appointed betters, our so-called elites who for one privileged reason or another found themselves in positions of power, actually do believe they are superior beings meant to tell the rest of us how to behave, speak, eat, drive and live. We must do all these things according to their specifications. They will never, ever, operate by the same rules they devise for the rest of us; they are privileged, smart and powerful. They don't need to abide by any rules including the Constitution. They are, as we see every day, above the law. The rest of us are well below it, subject to the whims of our government's institutions.

This is how they think, our Left. This is why Trump's rally last night in Orlando, if they deigned to watch, will have left them quivering in their boots with shock. Most probably did not watch, like the scene in *Rocky* when Apollo Creed is too busy to look at the video of Rocky in the meat locker when his trainer tries to get him to pay attention.

After all, with the media on their side, they were certain they would have brought the man down by now. Instead he is more popular than ever, and the press is looked upon with absolute scorn, for good reason. They, the NYT, WaPo, NBC, CBS, ABC, CNN, MSNBC discarded any semblance of objectivity long ago, long before Trump came upon the scene. They just became open about their bias once Trump was elected. No sentient person reasonably well-informed pays attention to any of those propaganda outlets. They are jokes, one and all, wastes of our time and the paper on which they are printed.

Trump has survived a nearly three-year onslaught of vicious attacks by his detractors. He has been set up, framed for things for which he is in no way guilty and still they insist he is guilty of something. He has been vilified 24/7 by the print and electronic media and still, many thousands of supporters showed up in Orlando to see him. And they were happy campers! Put a mic in the face of an anti-Trump person and what do you get? Hate, rage, and profanity. It has always been the left that is truly racist. The many, many African Americans who were in attendance in Orlando can all tell us that.

The Left has done everything in its power to destroy Trump and all they have done is expose their own hatefulness, intolerance and rage. They seem not to realize that all they have done is drive people to the man. He is a happy warrior who loves this country and its citizens above all. Happiness sells! Success sells! National security sells!

Record low unemployment is a good thing, as is a great economy. All this infuriates the Left. They so hate the man; they root for the nation to fail. But Trump is the Rocky of politics. He takes their beatings, gets battered and bruised by a despicable media but he never gives up. His speech Tuesday night was Rocky on the 72 stone steps of the Philadelphia Museum of Art to the strains of *Gonna Fly Now*.

In short, Trump is just getting started. Granted the fictional Rocky's beginnings were humble compared to Trump's, but then Rocky never had an entire movement dedicated to his annihilation. Despite the escalating idiocy of his detractors, Trump is a winner, a true champion of America."

–H/T Patricia McCarthy

https://www.**american**thinker.com/.../**does_anyone_doubt_that_ trump**_is_the _em**rocky**em_of_**american_politics**.html
Published with permission from the American Thinker.

Donald Trump as the Count of Monte Cristo

By Patricia McCarthy
April 19, 2019

"*The Count of Monte Cristo* by Dumas (1844) is the story of a good man of low birth, Edmond Dantès, who, at the hands of some high-born evil men, is sent to the island prison the Chateau d'If to get him out of the way. He spends thirteen years there before escaping. During those horrific years of torture and deprivation, he is schooled by another prisoner there, an Italian priest with knowledge of history, science, philosophy, languages, and the location of a vast treasure in gold. After he escapes, he recovers the gold and then, as a wealthy man, seeks to extract revenge on those who had him sent away to Hell on Earth.

This story comes to mind, given what Trump has endured these past three years when a cabal of noxious people set out to destroy him simply because they loathe the fact that he won the presidency. Who are these people? Hillary Clinton and her minions at Fusion GPS, Perkins-Coie, Comey and McCabe, Strzok and Page, et al. at the FBI, Rod Rosenstein, Sally Yates, and numerous others at the DOJ, John Brennan at the CIA, James Clapper at DIA. Noxious does not adequately describe how venal this bunch of treasonous people in positions of power truly are; they have destroyed the reputations of the agencies they once headed. As Dinesh D'Souza tweeted on Thursday, "[t]he left is powerful, dangerous and vicious. Large elements of it are also evil. But fortunately for us, it is also colossally stupid. We're watching the unraveling of one of its most stupid and evil operations right now."

The Mueller report has unequivocally cleared Trump of any collusion with Russia, but Mueller and his team of partisans left obstruction of justice up in the air, no doubt purposefully to keep CNN and MSNBC in business. The Mueller team obviously set out to create a path for the crazies in Congress to continue the witch hunt — and make no mistake: it was a witch hunt from the beginning. Trump has escaped the prison of the collusion investigation, but they are still coming after him. So on Thursday, the usual suspects declared themselves victors, claiming that the report vindicated their three years of reporting lies, rumors, leaks, etc. They want A.G. Barr to resign, asserting that he is sacrificing the country to be Trump's personal attorney, which is ridiculous on its face.

> *"Life is a storm, my young friend. You will bask in the sunlight one moment, be shattered on the rocks the next. What makes you a man is what you do when that storm comes. You must look into that storm and shout as you did in Rome. Do your worst, for I will do mine! Then the fates will know you as we know you."*
>
> Alexandre Dumas, *The Count of Monte Cristo*

Given the storm that Donald Trump has weathered over the past three years, and the strength with which he has suffered the slings and arrows of so many lesser men, one has to admire and respect his strength of character. Trump was likely, obviously, raised by a different sort of father from those of any of the political dynasties that have previously been sustained simply by their lofty names. The typical denizens of the D.C. establishment are an arrogant bunch: privileged, entitled, and self-important. There is little difference between the long-serving among them, left or right. Once they get there, most develop an uncanny thirst for power and the determination to keep it, no matter the cost to one's soul. They are like the prison guards at Chateau d'If. Once you have to spend most of your time fundraising or torturing prisoners, you are finished as a moral person.

Does Nancy Pelosi represent the residents of California? Not in the slightest. She has seen to it that her family has become fabulously wealthy thanks to her position in Congress. Pelosi could not care less about her constituents. She cares about one thing, one thing only: the power she has and seeks to retain. She has many like-minded friends who operate exactly as she does: Schumer, Feinstein, Nadler, Schiff, Swalwell, Cummings, Waters, et al. It is a long list of traitors to the people who elected them. Not only are they primarily self-interested, but they are determined to sabotage President Trump despite his remarkable success at rebooting the economy and slashing unemployment for all minority groups. They simply cannot abide an outsider like Trump succeeding so wildly on all fronts except immigration, the one issue with which they are determined to sabotage him. They are sabotaging all of us. They do not care about the rest of us.

So convinced are the Democrats that Trump could not have won legitimately that they unleashed their rage to unseat him. Yet he prevails, accomplishing more good for the nation than even Reagan did in his first two years. Tax cuts? No, they scream. But Trump's tax cuts have benefited all Americans, even Bernie Sanders. No to a wall to defend our southern border; that is the dumbest of all their tantrums. It is a crisis, purposefully devised by the Democrats, who hate Trump more than they love America. The crisis is exacerbated by the mysteriously funded far-left globalist groups, the drug cartels, and the human-traffickers with whom the Democrats have aligned themselves.

Our Democratic Party no longer has this country's best interests at heart; not even a little bit. The party is now fully socialist thus anti-capitalist and promotes open borders. Bernie Sanders and the rest of the Democrat presidential candidates so far mean to destroy the most vital economy in the world and to further destroy what was the best medical care in the world. They all want to abolish ICE, private insurance, cars, planes, anything fossil-fueled. Sanders and his pal Ocasio-Cortez, the party's brain trust, and their fans seem to have no grasp of the fact that oil and natural gas not only are the most basic elements of our economy, but have brought millions of people out of poverty and improved the quality of life across the planet. And we are not running out of it; the U.S. is now energy-independent.

All the forces of the Left have conspired to destroy a president they abhor. They loathe him because so many Americans love him. He has brought change — not the depressing transformational change Obama promised and did bring about. Trump has revitalized manufacturing, full employment, and pride in America. That is what infuriates the Left the most: pride in America. Our left, so wealthy and privileged, hates the nation whose Constitution and capitalism have made its members so rich and powerful, so formidable. These people mean to hamstring the rest of us while cementing their personal privilege. They have had nearly fifty years of tenured radicals to indoctrinate university students to their Marxist vision of what the U.S. should be. They have for as long owned the servile media that do their bidding with a vengeance. They must be stopped.

Donald Trump, the good guy, like Dumas's Edmond Dantès of *The Count of Monte Cristo*, has been investigatively shattered on the rocks for almost three years by the thoroughly disingenuous media and a hateful left. Dumas was on to something about humanity, as was Machiavelli: in politics, good people are the exception, not the rule. We have known for over two years that people with unelected power set out to undo the 2016 election by illegal and unconstitutional means. Obama was likely the mastermind of the insidious plot, or at least a partner to it; he had to approve the spying. The collective Left-media syndicate has conspired against Trump since before the election; just in case, these people developed an "insurance policy": that fake and ridiculous dossier paid for by the Clintons. Let us hope the truth will all be revealed, the instigators of this plot to unseat a president exposed and indicted for their crimes.

The fictional Edmond Dantès was set up by persons he thought were lifelong friends. They betrayed him for their own selfish purposes, just as so many on the Left and the right have betrayed Trump. Just as Dantès's self-aggrandizing, self-appointed superiors felt duty-bound to destroy a fine and brilliant man of "low birth," the NeverTrumps on both sides of the aisle are no better than Mondego and Villefort — amoral scoundrels who, in the book, each do suffer punishments that fit their crimes in the end.

Let us hope that as the truth of what those in the Obama administration who colluded with the Hillary Clinton campaign to impede a Trump candidacy and then presidency will suffer the well deserved consequences of their craven, blatantly illegal crime spree. That is what it was: a crime spree. The shocking thing is that they all believed they would get away with it, just as the villains of Dumas's tale assumed they would escape punishment for their crimes. They have done their worst!

As Dantès remarks while plotting his revenge, "I'm a count, not a saint." It is Trump's turn now to settle the score."

–H/T Patricia McCarthy

https://www.americanthinker.com/blog/2019/04/donald_trump_as_t
he_count_of_monte_cristo.html
Published with permission from the American Thinker.

Trump, America's eagle, soars alone

By Patricia McCarthy
May 28, 2019

"In a Chinese restaurant the other day, my fortune cookie message was this: *"Leaders are like eagles. They don't flock...you find them one at a time."* Not your usual fortune cookie note. No credit given for such a wise little sentence, probably because it is commonsense observation.

This little bit of universal truth made me smile. It was a timely reminder of how fortunate we are to have elected Donald Trump, not a member of any flock, which is why the D.C. establishment hates him so much. They are all of a flock. They think alike, act alike, do business alike, barter for favors in the same ways. For the most part, party identification is irrelevant. Most of the major players collude with each other. We conservatives must be grateful for the exceptions to the rule: Ron Johnson, Devin Nunes, Matt Gaetz, Chuck Grassley, Lindsey Graham, Jim Jordan, and Ted Cruz. There may be others momentarily out of mind, but the lesson of the quote is how rare real leaders actually are. We know now that both Mitt Romney and Paul Ryan would have been leaders but have since betrayed their stated conservative principles. Neither of them recognized Trump as the leader he is, and both have shamelessly sought to sabotage him. They are not the only ones. Justin Amash comes to mind, as do all the Republicans in Congress who quit because they thought Trump would be found guilty of the Russia collusion meme invented by that cabal of arrogant criminals in the Deep State who believed themselves to be above the law.

What has become of our American government? It long ago became an elite club of like-minded self-appointed elites who care only about preserving their own power and prestige. They care about enriching themselves, and they do indeed become very wealthy. Nancy Pelosi and Dianne Feinstein are among the richest members of Congress. Shouldn't we see their tax returns? What do they do for their constituents? Absolutely nothing. San Francisco, whence their political base springs, is a disaster of Democrat malfeasance. So is Los Angeles. Both cities are longtime Democrat strongholds. California is a one-party state, and it is Democrats who have singlehandedly destroyed it. Like Chicago, Detroit, and Baltimore, Democrat-run cities are like third-world entities, crime-ridden and corrupt. For decades, they've been run by flocks of "progressives" and have regressed into medieval bastions of the very rich versus the very poor. That's the way they like it, the middle class be damned.

The Left wants to be the boss, like the ridiculous Alexandria Ocasio-Cortez, to mandate how the rest of us live. The Left is a flock of wanna-be overlords. In their dreams, leftists revere Mao, Ho Chi Minh, and Stalin. Leftists such as Tom Friedman admire China and the way it is run; it's a communist dictatorship, and he writes for the NYT. The NYT is a member, perhaps the leader, of the flock. Its editors think they lead, but what they really do is propagandize as surely as Orwell's masters of a fictional universe manipulated its subjects. They lie. Orwell was more prescient than most authors; he understood how easily language could be corrupted, and he knew how catastrophic that corruption of language could be.

That Trump was elected is some kind of miracle. Somehow, enough people were awakened to the planned obliteration of American exceptionalism implemented by the Obama administration to get the man who promised to drain the swamp into the presidency. He is a leader who is like an eagle; he is one of a kind, a loner, an interloper into the world of American politics. For decades, he has been blasting what is wrong with our trade policies, etc. Now he is in a position to do something about the injustices all previous presidents have accepted as what

must be. And he is doing it. God bless the man who is not a member
of a flock, but our eagle who soars above the fetid swamp."

–H/T Patricia McCarthy

https://www.americanthinker.com/blog/2019/05/trump_americas_ea
gle_soars_alone.html#ixzz5pGXqoc7N
Published with permission from the American Thinker.

Why Trump Matters to Women

By Rose Tennent
July 18, 2019

"Carl Bernstein, of Watergate fame and not much else since, had a meltdown a few weeks ago, a common occurrence from the Left since Trump has taken office. While on CNN's *Reliable Sources* he called for a closer look into why people support Trump. He said,

> "No president in the history of the United States in 246 years has expressed the kinds of ideas and thoughts and undemocratic notions and authoritarian notions that he has. We need to start connecting these dots. What do people in the country think of this and why do they think and support him, no matter what he does, no matter how outrageous seemingly his conduct is."

Ever notice how the Left loves to accuse President Trump of "undemocratic" behavior? When pressed to explain exactly what those behaviors are, they've got nothing. But, I can help Carl out, particularly where women are concerned.

I know why Trump matters, especially to women and why we not only voted for him in 2016, but why we will vote for him again in 2020. We see him as a protector of those things we hold dear. We recognize that our long-held values are under attack from the Left. We believe he will defend those values. And this is really important: we want a man who keeps his promises. Trump did.

As women we took a close look at the state of our nation in 2016 and saw scars from years of neglect. Those who were charged with the preservation and protection of our Constitution failed us. Many in DC seemed to care more about their status and their pay-offs than they did about representing us and safeguarding our rights.

We saw just how much government became an industry, and as with all industries, it has its own set of interests and the desire for growth, increased power and influence. But unlike private sector industry, government produces no wealth. As a result, it must take its money by force, through taxes and regulations. When that wealth is redistributed, it is done so with a political purpose in mind. Contrary to what Hillary believed, we women saw that all by ourselves, without anyone "mansplaining" it to us. We saw it and it concerned us. We believed candidate Trump's promises to lower taxes and to massively reduce regulations, and then we watched it happen after he took office.

And while some on the Left and in the media attempted to shame us for our support of President Trump, we are not at all ashamed of his accomplishments. Yes, we are thrilled that female unemployment is currently at an over-60-year low – but that is not all we are thrilled about. It pleases us greatly that African American and Hispanic unemployment is at historic lows. Those of us who are mothers are thrilled that the youth unemployment is at a half-century low. Many of us are experiencing the best economy in our lifetime. And importantly, this administration respects and protects our veterans and supports law enforcement.

And it is extremely important to us that we have been successful on the world stage as well as at home. President Trump immediately withdrew us from the Trans Pacific Partnership, the (horrible) Iran Deal, and said *Au Revoir* to the scam that is the Paris Climate Accord.

Turns out, we women really have nothing to be ashamed about. We made a pretty damn good decision to elect Donald Trump. In the end, the media was successful only in strengthening our resolve when they vote shamed us. We feel emboldened as we go into 2020 as Women for Trump.

We recognize that Trump doesn't see the world through the same political eyes that the rest of us do. We find it refreshing that he is not an ideologue or a politician. We believe that he sees the Executive Branch as exactly that, and himself as the chief executive. Many of us believe that he considers this role as any executive would – with an eye toward a practical outcome rather than one that results in a political outcome. When we look at him we see something we haven't seen in a long time, a leader that simply loves this country — who believes in the greatness of this country, for which he makes no apologies. He is putting us first and is making government more accountable to the American people.

We believed him when he said he would Make America Great Again. So, what we really want as women when selecting representation, and as we celebrate 100 years of our constitutional right to take that selection to the ballot box in 2020, is the same guy who was able to "Make America Great Again" in order to "Keep America Great".

Hope this helps to connect some of those "dots" for Carl Bernstein." –
H/T Rose Tennent

**_Rose Tennent has been a prominent figure for twenty
years as a syndicated conservative political talk show host.
She is a frequent guest host for Sean Hannity's Radio Show
and has been a regular guest on FOX NEWS and serves on
the Advisory Board for Women For Trump Coalition. Rose
has authored a book called "Thanking Our Soldiers."_**

:

https://www.americanthinker.com/articles/2019/07/why_trump_matters_to_women.html#ixzz5uHToNkhl

Published with permission from the American Thinker.

Townhall *Daily*

Jews and Blacks for Trump

Wayne Allyn Root
Posted: Jul 21, 2019 12:01 AM

*The opinions expressed by columnists are their own and do
not represent the views of Townhall.com.*

"Blexit" and "Jexit" — those are the movements by conservative activist Candace Owens and me, respectively, to get blacks and Jews to leave the Democratic Party and support President Donald Trump.

Meanwhile, last week was another great week for President Trump. That must be why the Trump-hating national media have turned a Sunday tweet by the president into the biggest news headline in America. Trump's achievements were so fantastic in the past week that they had to once again use a tweet to try to destroy him. I'm betting you haven't heard a word about these Trump accomplishments in the mainstream news:

— The Dow crossed 27,000 for the first time in history, and the S&P 500 broke 3,000 for the first time.

— Food stamp participation is the lowest in 10 years (since Barack Obama).

— Border apprehensions reached the lowest level since March. Why? Because President Trump won the trade war with Mexican officials. They sent thousands of troops to their southern and northern borders. Mexico also agreed to keep the asylum seekers on its side of the border while their cases are being adjudicated. Trump won — again.

— The liberal 9th U.S. Circuit Court of Appeals handed Trump a victory on the issue of withholding federal funds from sanctuary cities.

— Trump announced new asylum rules that force illegals to apply in another country first. No more open borders. Middle-class Americans will applaud this news.

But I saved the best for last. I'll bet you didn't hear this one on the evening news. Robert Johnson, the founder of Black Entertainment Television, shocked the world; he's disillusioned with Democrats.

The first black billionaire in America's history is a lifelong Democrat donor. He supported Hillary in 2016. Johnson told CNBC the Democratic Party has moved "too far to the left," and so, "The message of some of the programs that Democrats are pushing are not resonating with the majority of the American people."

Johnson praised Trump's handling of the economy. He gave Trump credit for the lowest black unemployment ever. He admitted Trump's tax cuts led to this booming economy. He gave Trump a grade of A-plus for the economy. Johnson's summation: "I give the president a lot of credit for moving the economy in a positive direction that's benefiting a large amount of Americans."

Wait for the clincher: This lifelong Democrat says he isn't supporting any Democrat for president in 2020.

The point of Owens' Blexit" and my Jexit is not to produce a majority of blacks and Jews for Trump. We know that can't happen overnight. But just a few percentage points in Trump's direction will turn 2020 into a Trump electoral landslide. That's the point of Blexit and Jexit. And trust me, it's happening. Democrats are scared to death.

https://townhall.com/columnists/wayneallynroot/2019/07/21/jews_and_blacks_for_trump_n2550319
Published with permission from Wayne Allyn Root.

Trump the deviant

By Michael Smith
June 12, 2019

"President Trump is a deviant, of that there is no argument. On that, Democrats, NeverTrumpers and Trump supporters all can agree – and by "deviant", I simply mean that he varies from the accepted norms. Now whether you see this as a good thing or a bad thing is a matter worthy of discussion, but one thing is true, Trump represents a significant departure from presidential culture of the past 50 years.Trump's deviancy threatens the left because it shows people there is another, more direct way to get things done than the mutated and metastasized puffery practiced by the powdered wig disciples of a process of indirect diplomacy straight out of the perfumed courts of 18th century Europe.

It's a problem for the Left due to the pseudo-realistic world they have created — and have trained generations of pre-pubescent progressives it is a world in which they should expect to live. It's a world where there are such things as female penises and menstruating male vaginas, a world where any people can "identify" as anything their deluded minds can conceive, and society as a whole is not only expected to accept that choice but must celebrate it in the loudest of voices. It is a world in which weak beta males establish the boundaries for masculinity and butch masculine females are expected to be the alpha.

In the Marvel comic and cinematic universes, Dr. Strange can create a "mirror universe" where sorcery can be practiced without changing the real world — that's where the progressive sorcerers live — the mirror universe.

Thank goodness, this leftist world is a "mirror" creation that doesn't exist. President Trump inhabits a world where people are plainspoken and there are consequences. I'm not surprised he told Mexico to straighten up and respect our borders by respecting theirs. It's what serous people do — nobody has time for parenthetical comments directed at third parties in the hope the real target can decode the message.

During the primary season, I was one of many who called out Trump's frequent flirtation with bankruptcies as a negative — but bankruptcies exist in the real world. In the private sector, bad decisions and unexpected conditions have consequences, consequences that those who have spent a lifetime in government (Joe Biden and Bernie Sanders) will never experience — because if there are people, there are always taxes. Ayn Rand said:

> A businessman cannot force you to buy his product; if he makes a mistake, he suffers the consequences; if he fails, he takes the loss. A bureaucrat forces you to obey his decisions, whether you agree with him or not—and the more advanced the stage of a country's statism, the wider and more discretionary the powers wielded by a bureaucrat. If he makes a mistake, you suffer the consequences; if he fails, he passes the loss on to you, in the form of heavier taxes.

It's not just that progressives and NeverTrumpers hate the President personally (and they certainly do hate him with the heat of a thousand suns), it is that he bends the line of progression toward a world that for fifty years they assiduously worked to create (and control) — and he bends it at a ninety degree angle.

What are they going to do with all those drones they spent so much time to indoctrinate in government schools if Trump exposes the lie of the progressive mirror universe?"

-H/T Michael Smith

https://www.americanthinker.com/blog/2019/06/trump_the_deviant.html
Published with permission from the American Thinker.

Trump is the most law-abiding president ever!

By Patricia McCarthy
May 22, 2019

"The Left in America hates, loathes, and despises President Trump. Why? Because he is not one of them, and he won. He was not supposed to win. How could he have prevailed? The leftists had it wrapped up. All the polls said so, just as they said climate change Labor candidate Shorten was a shoe-in in Australia. Oops.

Trump's victory in the 2016 election was a cataclysmic shock to the establishment whose members believed, with every fiber of their being, that they ran things, all things governmental. The denizens of D.C. do not pay much attention to party affiliation. They all abided by the Beltway rules: never rock the boat. Get elected, do the bidding of your donors, and get rich. That's it for the bulk of them, but thankfully not all of them. Those who challenge the status quo will be dispensed with in short order, one way or another. And if they manage to stay, like Bush the younger, they will be pilloried day in and day out.

Bush played by the rules; he did not fight back. He took their slings and arrows like a man, so they said. He let them eviscerate him, let them claim he was an illegitimate president. He was a good man, but he played by their rules. It never occurred to him to do otherwise.

Bush's subservience gave way to Obama, the very worst president in modern U.S. history. He came to office as a man who hated this nation. He won by promising to "fundamentally transform America." That promise should have been a wake-up call to all Americans, but instead, it lulled his fans into a sort of trance, like teenage girls who fell for Elvis Presley in the 1950s.

Neither reason nor intelligence had anything to do with Obama's elections. He easily manipulated the ignorant and just as easily wooed the elites with their own desperation to matter, to be celebrated as smart, savvy and not racist. But they are, and have always been, the racists, which is why they were such willing dupes, desperate not to be exposed. The Democratic Party is not only racist; it is increasingly openly anti-Semitic.

Enter Donald Trump. The man does not have a racist bone in his body. Any simple search of his background in N.Y. will prove he is not a race-conscious man. He pays no attention to skin color. He loves and supports Israel; his daughter converted to Judaism. He adores his grandchildren. But the Left's mission is to paint him as a racist and anti-Semite. Projection is the Left's most obvious knee-jerk response to everything leftists hate and fear.

What to do? Investigate Trump to the ends of the earth. There must be something of which they can find him guilty. He is wealthy and enormously successful. He has employed hundreds of thousands of people over the years. Surely, they can find him guilty of some crime. Aren't all rich people guilty of crimes? How else did they become rich? Trump, they think, is a criminal because his has been successful in several realms. He must have cheated. That is how the Left thinks. The Left is all about envy, never respect for achievement.

So leftists invented, out of whole cloth, a crime: he "colluded' with Russia to defeat Hillary Clinton, the most corrupt candidate ever to seek the presidency. Unable to accept her and their own defeat, they devised a grand plot, a narrative they were certain would bring this good man down. They hired spies, all from Western allies, and inserted them into the lives of people they thought they could exploit. The Clintons commissioned and paid for the ridiculous dossier that every professional intel person knew upon first glance was phony.

It is the arrogance of the Left that brings it down every time. Leftists truly believe that everyone outside their bubble is a deplorable idiot when in fact it is they who are the morons. Trump had their number from day one.

Now, after two and a half years of investigation of all things Trump, including his family, which was just an attempt to cover up the Left's own crimes, the pseudo-investigation is over. Even Mueller and his band of Trump-hating Beltway lawyers could not find anything criminal with which to charge the man. This makes him the most investigated, cleared, and thus the most honest and above board president in U.S. history.

The Democrats cannot accept this fact and have descended into a sewer of their own making. They are floundering about, issuing nonsensical subpoenas to persons peripheral to the president, all because they can't accept the results of the Mueller report. They are grasping at volume 2 of the report, as though it were useful for their ends. It's not. Trump can't be charged with obstructing an investigation that began with no crime and ended with no crime. He was rightfully angry by the entire setup, which he knew from day one was fallacious, but he never impeded Mueller.

Now all Americans know, whether or not the Democrats among them can accept it, that Trump never colluded with Russia to win the election. Hillary did, the DNC did, the Obama administration did, all with malice aforethought. The entire enterprise has been the most treasonous action ever taken by an opposition party. It is the worst political scandal in U.S. history. And how has it ended? The insanity of the democrats like Nadler and Schiff is palpable. They are desperate, and their desperation is showing.

But the bottom line is that Trump has weathered the most intense, malicious investigation in American history and come up clean. We are a fortunate nation to have elected this man to lead us. He is the best president since Reagan, and most of us are grateful, even those who cannot utter their gratitude aloud. Polls be damned. They are a tool of the Left, rarely a legitimate reflection of the aspirations of the people."

–H/T Patricia McCarthy

https://www.americanthinker.com/blog/2019/05/trump_is_the_most
_lawabiding_president_ever.html
Published with permission from the American Thinker.

Love Trump without overlooking his faults

By Richard Jack Rail
March 31, 2019

"An unfortunate trend seems to be developing among Trump-supporters. Many of these seem to think the president has no faults, or at least none that merits mention in any discussion of American politics today. This is simply bad thinking; as good as Trump is, both as a man and as a president, he has as many faults as anyone — mainly a big mouth that unnecessarily keeps opposition anger white-hot.

This can be fun to watch, as when he snubbed the White House Correspondents' dinner. The shrewish leftists were just sure he had no choice but to go, and they planned to barbecue him. Instead, he forced many of them out of their white ties and tuxes to attend his rally that same night in another state among the very rubes and hicks the snotty Left so detests.

When he first came on the scene as a serious presidential contender, I relished Trump's combativeness. I still enjoy it when he shoves their viciousness right back in their faces, and I positively howl with delight when they get their heads handed to them. I voted for Donald Trump and wish I could have voted for him a hundred times, a thousand times. But he's not a Democrat; it's they who do that.

There are times when indifference to the other side's rage is the right thing. They *need* their wrongness and their wrongheadedness rubbed in their faces from time to time. But doing it all the time risks igniting the demented, the Hodgkinsons who go on murderous rampages. Rubbing it in probably pushes their unreasonable hatred into areas of the unbalanced psyche where that hatred might not go if not goaded into it.

More fundamentally, it's simply unrealistic to pretend your leader is spotless, blameless, and perfectly clean. The Idiot Left does that, and we need to leave its members to it. Donald Trump is the right president for our time and one of the best America has ever had, and it's because he's firmly grounded in reality. Our judgments of him also need to be that way. I'd wager that Trump himself would agree with this assessment, though it won't change his behavior. Besides despising the lying press for 30 years, he is by nature a scrapper who fights to win.

We can enjoy watching him win battles without doubting that he often goes too far for his (or our) own good. It's one of those "bad news and good news" things where the former overwhelms the latter without erasing it. So shrug your shoulders. We need to (perhaps silently) acknowledge it to keep our own judgments real."

-H/T Richard Jack Rail

https://www.americanthinker.com/blog/2019/03/love_trump_without_overlooking_his_faults.html
Published with permission from the American Thinker.

Trump is no Racist

By Taylor Lewis
July 20, 2019

"Shelley called poets the unacknowledged legislators of the world. Auden, who was never as full of sauce as some prosody scribes, rejoined mordantly: "'The unacknowledged legislators of the world,' describes the secret police, not the poets."

Auden's portentous bon mot is truer now than when he wrote it, albeit with one difference. "The secret police" no longer refers to collectivist stormtroopers tracking down intrigants but, rather, something subtler but no less perverse. Don't misinterpret my meaning: The target is still the grey matter between your ears. Only the remedy for offense has changed. Rather than convince you of your crime with the snub-nosed barrel of a Korovin, the preferred weapon is language corruption in service to emotional manipulation.

The most galling example of this tactic of late has been the high dudgeon reaction to President Trump's suggestion that four congresswoman, all Democratic women of color, go back to their country of origin before describing the United States in calumnious terms. Trump's half-joking entreaty, delivered, as usual, through the hair-trigger forum of Twitter, was all but ignored for its substance. "Why don't they go back and help fix the totally broken and crime infested places from which they came," Trump suggested to the progressive posse known as the Squad, following up with an additional directive. "Then come back and show us how...it is done."

Strictly speaking, Trump's proposition contained one erratum: his mistaking three of the four lawmakers' homeland for anywhere other

than America. Rep. Omar Ilhan of Minnesota is the only member of the far-left cadre to not be born on U.S. soil, hailing originally from Somalia. The rest are American, born and bred.

Still, it doesn't take a four-year degree from Trump University to grasp what the President was expatiating: that Rep. Omar, who comes from a war-torn, anarchic piece of sod we generously called a nation-state, should, perhaps, show a little gratitude for the country that took her and her family in.

Call it a knee-jerk nationalism. Call it jingoistic. Call it reactionary, graceless, unwelcoming, or just plain mean-spirited. Trump's remark, however, wasn't racist, at least by the term's essential definition. This is a pedantic point, but a necessary one, because the term itself – racism — is so irresponsibly bandied about that it has effectively been nerfed of the moral force it once contained.

To repeat, Trump's tweets were not racist. Nothing of what the President said referenced skin color or indicated racial superiority. He was speaking only in terms of nationality. Somalia is majority black, but, by liberals' own lights, the U.S. is demographically dynamic, progressively losing its white-majority character. Somali refugees aren't tainting our already muddied racial pool.

That hasn't stopped most major media outlets from labeling Trump's comments "racist" as a linguistic truth in headlines. CNN, PBS, and CBS didn't hesitate to characterize the tweets as racially malicious. The only holdout was NPR V.P. Keith Woods, who propounded the idea that journalists should "not be in the business of moral labeling in the first place." Poor Keith clearly hasn't logged on to Twitter lately.

Reading racism into Trump's tweets isn't about applying the word's meaning to the President's language. When journalists call his rhetorical suggestion of self-deportation racist, what they're really doing is conjecturing about his motivation. "President Trump wishes America was whiter, hence his urging of non-white immigrants to leave," is the through line of thought that occurred in many reporters' heads. It's the assumption of thoughtcrime, the kind of practice that would be home in a Philip K. Dick-imagined dystopia or any real-life oppressive regime.

There is no semantical point to all of this. It's a smear exercise that makes use of language's slippery essence to invoke emotion. That's why a CNN reporter asked large retailers like Target and Walmart to weigh in on the President's comments. No American business wants to be seen as soft on racism, or even tacitly supportive of racial bias. So, their corporate H.R. division issues a bland statement about not countenancing racism. Newsrooms leap into a flurry of action, producing headlines about how the Target dog just took a bite out of Trump's rampant bigotry.

The entire production is classified as "news," which is another term that increasingly lacks precise definition. Charles Cooke calls the national press "obsequious asbestos salesmen" but he's being too kind. Asbestos has a purpose in construction. The dreck journalists produce today is deconstructive, tearing at the already feeble foundation of our shared language and understanding.

"[T]o think clearly is a necessary first step toward political regeneration," Orwell wrote. When our elected leaders, or journalists charged with keeping them aboveboard, abuse language to solicit charged reactions, they're inhibiting our ability to see and think objectively.

At this point, every Republican president since Calvin Coolidge has been called racist. The term has already become watered down to the point of irrelevancy. You can thank the serial users of the word for draining it of its potency. Would that pedants, not poets or the police, were the unacknowledged legislators of the world."

–H/T Taylor Lewis

https://tmp.americanthinker.com/articles/2019/07/trump_is_no_racist.html
Published with permission from the American Thinker.

Reminder: Trump Is Only Human

By Lloyd Marcus
April 14, 2019

"Despite a billion dollars' worth of negative press to destroy Trump before he was elected — over 500,000 lying articles claiming that Trump colluded with Russia and the Deep State's $30-million illegal investigation, Trump has miraculously survived. Incredibly, Trump has stayed on offense, laser-focused on making America great again. The treasonous anti-Trump coalition is frustrated, hatefully consumed with creating Kryptonite to take down this political Superman.

While he has performed like a man of steel, Trump is only human. Ninety-two percent of media reporting on Trump is negative. How much abuse can this man take? It is vitally important that We the People assure President Trump that we have his back. Tea Party Express launching "Tea Party for Trump" is divinely timed.

Sarah Palin was a conservative warrior, an answer to the prayers of Christians, conservatives, and Republicans. I still remember the joy and excitement I felt hearing Sarah Palin's acceptance speech to run as John McCain's vice president. Palin was bright, bold, and beautiful, unembarrassed to stand up for principles and values that have made America great.

Immediately after Palin accepted the V.P. nomination, the American left launched a no-holds-barred campaign to destroy her. Palin's entire family, including her Down syndrome toddler son, were high-tech lynched by fake news media. Every word out of Palin's mouth was spun to brand her crazy, stupid, or racist.

This is exactly the same tactic Democrats and their minions have used to keep Trump's approval below 50%. The same way leftists viciously attacked Palin's family, actor Peter Fonda said Trump's 12-year-old son should be caged with pedophiles to be gang-raped. Whose family could endure such vile, relentless hate? The American left decreed commenting on Obama's family out of bounds while declaring it open season on attacking the families of Palin and Trump.

Despite the Mueller Report concluding that Trump did not collude with Russia to steal the presidency from Hillary, NeverTrumps and Republicans maintain a safe distance from Trump, halfheartedly supportive of his America first agenda. Once again, I am reminded of our side's disloyalty to Sarah Palin.

Making sure that none of the excrement fake news media showered upon Palin splashed on them, conservatives and Republicans distanced themselves from Sarah Palin. Word in conservative and Republican circles was that Palin had become politically toxic. Frustrated, I thought, "So this is how we treat our friends and courageous warriors?"

Trump does not play by any of Washington, D.C. elitists' rules. Trump drives them nuts.

The assault on Palin pales in comparison to what Democrats, fake news media, Hollywood, NeverTrumps, RINOs, and the Deep State are doing to president Trump. Every day, this man awakens to face a tsunami of media lies, distortions, and the narrative that Americans hate his guts. None of Trump's remarkable, unprecedented achievements for We the People is reported.

Trump is despised by the American left because he is effectively blocking its mission to transform America away from the vision of our Founding Fathers, rooted in biblical principles. Another reason Trump is despised is because he is a man of the people. Leftists and political elites are shallow, ruled by surface appearances.

For example, New York Times columnist David Brooks absurdly said seeing Obama's perfectly creased pants told him Obama would be a great president. Obama was a master of what we in the black community describe as "jive talkin'." Whenever Obama gave one of his incomprehensible, rambling answers, his fake news media sycophants were enraptured. They would interpret the brilliance of Obama's superior intellect to us commoners.

The Bible says, "Man looks on the outward appearance, but the Lord looks on the heart" (1 Samuel 16:7). When Trump speaks, leftists and political elites are appalled. In contrast, We the People see, hear, and connect with Trump's heart — his love for America and his sincere commitment to serving her best interest.

God has a hedge of protection around Trump. Millions of Christians are praying for him, which I believe is the source of Trump's remarkable strength, endurance, and focus. Still, Trump is only human. Anti-Trump resisters relentlessly attempt to character-assassinate him 24/7.

Trump needs to hear daily that we appreciate his courage and that we are solidly standing shoulder to shoulder with him. We must help Trump keep America great in 2020.

Lyrics from the song "One Day at a Time": "I'm only human. I'm just a man. Just give me the strength to do every day what I have to do. Lord, help me today; show me the way one day at a time." –H/T Lloyd Marcus

Lloyd Marcus,
The Unhyphenated American

https://www.americanthinker.com/articles/2019/04/reminder_trump_is_only_human.html
Published with permission from the American Thinker.

Townhall *Daily*

Shock and Awe, Trump Style

Sheriff David Clarke (Ret.)
Posted: Jul 19, 2019 1:00 PM

The opinions expressed by columnists are their own and do not represent the views of Townhall.com.

Source: AP Photo/Carolyn Kaster

"President Donald Trump delivered a haymaker to the bully freshman House of Representative class of Democrats when he told them to shut up or get out. He took an old political phrase and served it with blue-collar articulation—half-cooked and cold. You know the phrase, "America, Love it or Leave it." Remember when it was on bumper stickers and buttons? It was a phrase to remind Anti-American subversives who were at the time not just critical of America but were intent on destroying the very fabric of our country. Well, sadly, they are back and will destroy our county—if we let them.

A group of malcontent snotty-nosed freshmen lawmakers in the House of Representatives are pushing an anti-American agenda. But they are up against an opponent who hits back. In a series of recent tweets, President Trump unleashed—let's say—the MOAT (Mother Of All Tweets). Then he doubled down on it the next day. Any other GOP politician would have walked it back, apologized and gone into seclusion until the backlash subsided. Not Trump. These America haters are up against a president who loves America and defends and praises the U.S. everywhere he goes, and at every chance he gets, to do so.

What these freshmen brats forget is that Trump is not afraid to color outside the lines of traditionally defined behavior for presidents that go back to the founding of this nation. He has redefined the office of the president. He has reformulated what it means to be a Republican and a conservative. Trump fights back like no Republican ever has. When the left throws rocks at him, he picks those rock up and hurls them right back. He fights with very few reliable fighters on his side on Capitol Hill. Most GOPers are still afraid of the left and choose to stay close to the shore and roll over. They say they are not a "Trump-kind-of-Republican." Someone needs to remind the left that Trump doesn't just counterpunch, he punches first when strategically advantageous and forces Democrats to respond to him. People love it, and Trump knows it.

Consequently, the left has defined new rules of engagement for themselves about what they can get away with—what they can say or do in the political arena and with impunity. They get plenty of cover from their accomplices in the liberal media. The editorial boards of *The New York Times, Washington Post, USA Today* and the anchors of CNN and MSNBC and network television carry their water. They control the language. It has given them an advantage in political discourse. They can say whatever they want about whoever they want and without political liability.

These folks on the left refuse to denounce the use of political violence by Antifa. Really? As if it is that difficult to see the violence these miscreants routinely use. The left has also called Trump Hitler, accused him of criminal behavior where there is no evidence, Democrat Representative Rashida Tlaib twice said at rallies, *...we are gonna impeach that mother-* (then dropped an f-bomb) referring to Trump. Since the day Trump was elected, the left has engaged not in traditional political opposition but downright raw resistance. They have mistreated his family and lie that he puts kids in cages at detention facilities. From the day he was sworn in as the 45th president, he has fought back and in unconventional ways. And he is winning. He knows the enemy, and he identifies it to the American people. Then he goes after them. His never-back-down style has Democrats and the left pulling their hair out. I love it. None of the tactics they have used in the past to get rid of political opposition or Republicans has worked. They can't get rid of him. He never tires of the fight and he won't. Not only has his base had it with the constant aggression against Trump; there is no doubt in my mind that even people not politically active have had it too. They are tired of hearing about white privilege, reparations and the myth of their implicit bias against minorities. It's Trump's turn to feed the beast like the left does with their rabid base when they call every American not swallowing their agenda, a racist, homophobe, Islama-phobe, xenophobe or misogynist. And he did not disappoint with his tweets. What the left does not understand about Trump's base is that they live vicariously through him. When they see him mistreated, they feel mistreated. It's that basket of deplorables moment all over again. In other words, we are all Trump.

Silently many Trump supporters understood Trump's blue-collar way of telling those who hate America to love it or leave it. Politically only Trump could say it the way he did and not lose voters. Many of his supporters nodded to themselves in agreement.

There is an emotional connection between President Trump and his supporters that mirrors the emotional support between black voters and Obama. Good, bad, indifferent and whether Obama was wrong on something or not, black voters were not abandoning Obama. As with Trump supporters, we won't leave him either. There is nothing you can do to change that; he's our guy. Are we clear? "

–H/T Sheriff David Clarke

https://townhall.com/ - Columnists/Shock and Awe, Trump Style
H/T Townhall Daily

Diogenes's search is over

By Bill King
May 11, 2019

"If Diogenes were alive today, his endless search for an honest man would bring him to 1600 Pennsylvania Avenue. And, whether it be at midnight or at the brightest noon, Diogenes would meet the most honest man in American political life, Donald Trump.

Need proof? Just sedate Mueller and his 16 black-hearted marauders, then listen to their anguish about their two-year persecution of the Man of Orange Hair.

There is now no doubt that there was no Russian collusion predicate driving Mueller's endless search for any crime, committed anytime and anywhere, by Trump. How else can one explain Mueller's vile actions in putting Flynn, Manafort, Corsi, Stone (just to name a handful of Trump-connected individuals) on the rack to torture out false statements about unlawful and illicit conduct by Queens-raised Trump? One can only imagine the utter disbelief by Mueller and his henchmen when they turned cowardly-lion Cohen inside-out, fully expecting some corrupt deed by Trump to be shaken loose — and found not a scintilla of actionable evidence.

After using tactics and stratagems employed by Iron-Curtain Lavrenti Beria, including examining Trump's tax returns and financial statements and investigating Trump's kids, the Mueller miscreants came up with nothing! Why? These wretched souls, so morally corrupt and dishonest in their own actions and thoughts, were incapable of considering that anyone, especially a billionaire like Trump, would possess a steady moral and ethical compass to guide him through life.

Donald J. Trump is one of the most transparent, sincere, and honest public figures in modern American history. With a rock-steady backbone, love of family, and his sincerest belief in the greatness of America, Trump has suffered the calumnies and filth hurled at him daily since becoming POTUS on November 8, 2016. Does anyone among us believe he could survive in reputation or sanity from such a relentless battering? I know I could not. History will reflect that President Trump withstood the search-and-destroy storm unleashed upon him by treacherous Obama administrative officials, the evil Queen Hillary, and soulless mainstream journalists — that Trump stood firm at the precipice and prevented our constitutional republic from plummeting into a socialist abyss."

-H/T **Bill King**

https://www.americanthinker.com/blog/2019/05/diogenes_search_is_over.html
Published with permission from the American Thinker.

Finally, conservatives have a street fighter as president

By Steve Grammatico
August 24, 2019

"Has there been a president in living memory who relishes a fight more than Trump? I don't think so. That is a major reason why he remains popular with conservatives and has seen his favorability ratings rise.

Sure, I like President Trump's actions on job-killing regulations, tax relief, border security, energy independence, military funding, judicial appointments, and so on. But what really invigorates me and millions of other EverTrumpers is that he is fearless — impervious to attacks by his adversaries and merciless in responding to them.

Source: AP Photo/Carolyn Kaster

Trump is an oddity: a Republican president who stands up to the Left's defamations and brickbats and returns fire. His prickly personality is one driving force; another is Twitter, the social media megaphone he uses to bypass the legacy media's censors.

Especially gratifying to his base is Trump's war on PC and his refusal to be restrained by liberals' standards of what constitutes acceptable speech. Go after him and your race or ethnicity will not protect you from his wrath. House Oversight Chairman Elijah Cummings learned this lesson recently, to his chagrin. In a nation where Trumpers are afraid to wear a MAGA cap in public, who else would dare to call out a civil rights icon on conditions in his district?

The drumbeat of criticism and calumny directed at the president by his political opponents and the media have had no discernible physical or emotional effect on him, except perhaps to make him more energetic and determined, and his tweets more sharply worded and devastating. Meanwhile, those who spew venom in their rage against the man are diminished. (See the latest comment by Rob "Meathead" Reiner.) As he fends off with alacrity the daily assaults on his character, intelligence, and motives, supporters like me are heartened.

TDS hard cases appear to believe the deplorables will desert Trump in droves after he is impeached and in the dock. Wishful thinking. Not only will the base remain loyal, his favorability will continue to increase when independents and fence sitters tune in and get a load of insufferable Democratic prosecutors trying to make something of nothing.

More reasonable Trump haters hope a Senate trial tarnishes Trump and his presidency leading up to November 2020. More likely, voters would punish Democrats for inflicting a show trial on the nation.

In their efforts to convince America Trump is the problem, the perpetrators of the Deep State coup and their allies are buttressing the case that Trump is the solution to what ails America.

When the president arguably goes over the top, I might shake my head a little, and then I forget it. I've waited a long time for a street fighter on my side of the political divide to occupy the Oval Office. It's finally happened, and I couldn't be more pleased".

-H/T Steve Grammatico is the author of You Hear Me, Barack?: PC-Free Conservative Satire. He blogs

**at You Hear Me, Barack? A Reposi-
tory of Conservative Satire, where
he's reprised from the book another piece of satire on Hapless Joe
Biden.**

https://www.americanthinker.com/.../**finally_conservatives_have
_a_street_ fighter_as_president**.html
Published with permission from the American Thinker.

Victor Davis Hanson on *The Case for Trump*

By Terry Scambray
June 16, 2019

The Case for Trump, Victor Davis Hanson. Basic Books, 2019. 372 pp.

"As the title suggests, *The Case for Trump,* balances a clinical approach to our currently incendiary politics alongside a brief for Donald Trump's presidency. Of course, the success or failure of this attempt is a subjective matter though it seems to me that any reader of this book of whatever political stripe would concede that, for its length, it is thorough if not encyclopedic in its presentation of facts and its historical depth.

All of which is not surprising in that Victor Davis Hanson, occupies a unique position among the commentariat: he is a classical scholar, professor, historian, novelist, political, cultural commentator and farmer in California's central valley while maintaining a residence in Palo Alto where he is a senior fellow at the Hoover Institution on the Stanford campus. He is also a visiting professor at Hillsdale College in Michigan while spending appreciable time overseas.

One can see that his distinctly varied experiences are part of why he remains an engaging thinker and which makes all of the 372 pages of this book fly by. In a word, the book is a deliciously informative and an eminently readable take on the Trump ship of state as it tries to navigate around the depth charges laid by the treacherous deep state armada and a giddy and obtuse paparazzi.

Dr. Hanson's opening chapter is his longest, wherein he demonstrates that by 2016 the traditional vision of "the two Americas" had ossified into mere "stale sloganeering." As he puts it, "Trump did not create these divides. He merely found existing sectarianism politically useful, and, like President Obama, he far more adroitly leveraged it than had prior Republican nominees. "

Yes, the educated, progressive, technocracies in the costal blue states had turned their backs on America's interior and in looking overseas became increasingly smug in their cosmopolitanism while showcasing their empathy for the hapless in destitute places outside America. Of course, this coastal blue state cult is shared by Illinois and other interior states, depending on issues and candidates, where empathy is also on display for "people of color" and other victims of America's presumed institutional and incipient phobias.

Certainly the most recent Republican presidential candidates, Messieurs McCain and Romney, saw this divide but neither had the requisite body armor, aka thick enough skin, to expose themselves to the heavy media artillery that would be wheeled around and directed at them if they risked any association with the Buchanan, pitchfork branch of the party, "the isolationist wing," "the America Firsters," the un-glamorous white working class, "the deplorables," "the smelly Wall Mart shoppers" and on and on, the invective lexicon of the Left being as endless as it is predictable.

However, being partially a media creation himself as well as having extensive experience with politicians, Trump went full speed ahead and damned the torpedoes aimed at him. Thus, he wasn't afraid to tailor his appeal to this disdained constituency (which he now owns), notwithstanding that Joe Biden is currently channeling Joe the Plumber as he tries to woo this group in the run-up to 2020.

Hanson drills deeper by noting that Trump knew that "a good job was the wellspring alone from which followed a stable two-parent family, home ownership, and a sense of confidence and pride." Certainly, "white, lower middle class pathology was often known to the Left in the manner of a stiff, dissected frog reeking of formaldehyde" in studies by intellectuals like Charles Murray. Though, as Hanson continues, "Before Trump, few politicians saw an opening in defending the forgotten working class of the interior and few politicians knew it firsthand, much less saw it as merited or even useful in the political sense."

Were others blinded by their own predilections? As Hanson reveals, "college-educated whites do *not* make up 36% of the electorate" as analysts indicated; this constituency made up only 30% and was outnumbered by non-college working class whites.

Hanson describes the cult of progressivism as driven by "the white elite signaling their disgust at the 'white privilege' of the disintegrating middle class as a means of exempting their own quite genuine white privilege of insider contacts, professional degrees, wealth, inheritance, and influence." Trump tapped into this lower middle-class disgust provoked by such haughty virtue signaling by those in the media, Hollywood, corporations, academia and government.

Prior to the 2012 election, Hanson was chauffeured through southern Michigan by a retired autoworker who let loose with a stream-of-consciousness trashing of President Obama. After which, Hanson remarked, "Well, I guess that you'll be voting for Romney." The man bristled: "Romney? Geez, Romney came to Michigan wearing his wing tips with starched jeans." Likewise, Hillary's hamming it up as Aunt Jemima with her, *"I don't feel no ways tired. . ."* mantra also made her merely one among the many of our political actors. By contrast Donald

Trump was not a character in search of himself; he unselfconsciously played himself in his trademark business suit punctuated by that long red tie resembling the extended tongue that he is always prepared to stick out at his tormentors.

As Professor Hanson writes, "Globalization had flattened the hinterland, had long ago appropriated or Xeroxed America's interior wealth, manufacturing, and industrialization." Indeed, economists for the last 40 years have insisted that America must adjust to a flat earth leveled by "free trade" while correspondingly big picture historians have, some gleefully, predicted the leveling of America to a position as merely one among many in "the family of nations."

But some things change and some things don't. Farmer and historian Hanson knows that all too well. Similarly as Trump shows in *The Art of the Deal*, he is not overly impressed by "intellectuals" with their unmoored, free floating notions, the consequences of which they invariably exempt themselves from. In fact, people require jobs in order to be people, just as countries, especially America as the world's backbone, need manufacturing and agriculture as well as high tech and great universities and, perhaps, even think tanks, in order to be a country.

Early on Hanson quotes Henry Kissinger's remark: "I think Trump may be one of those figures in history who emerges from time to time to mark the end of an era and to force it to give up its old pretense." Whether for good or ill, Trump has challenged the world's status quo in which the United States is seen as the banker, policeman, scapegoat, Mother Teresa, Uncle Sam, a place where wealthy third world kleptocrats send their children to be educated and their poor to be provided for, and the place most everyone aspires to get into one way or another.

Of course, a transformational individual like Trump will necessarily draw a diversity of detractors. The last part of the book explores that great chain of beings, those scampering mice-like Lilliputians in the media and the deep state trying to tie Trump down. Ben Rhodes, for example, a big shot in the Obama administration, is the brother of the president of CBS News and was married to a foreign policy advisor to

Barbara Boxer, Ann Norris, who was also a high muck-a-muck in the State Dept. Dr. Hanson reveals legions of like links.

What's juicy about Mr. Rhodes is that he is not shy about revealing his contempt for his media mouthpieces. As he puts it, "The average reporter that we talk to is twenty-seven years old. That's a sea change. They literally know nothing. [Thus] We created an echo chamber." So too MIT's Jonathan Gruber openly bragged that he had "hoodwinked dumb Americans" in getting Obamacare passed. No surprise then that the negative reporting by the major networks on Trump reached 91% over one three month period.

Such institutionalized megaphones can drown out the many re-markable milestones that Trump has achieved and that Hanson charts, milestones like: unprecedented 3% yearly economic growth with quar-terly growth climbing as high as 4.1%; major stock indexes as of the end of April at record highs; highest ever recorded Hispanic and black employment; lowest percentage of the population ever on food stamps; business investment up by 40% in the first quarter of 2018; overall 18 month economic growth faster than any comparable period during President Obama's tenure.

Other Trump initiatives, as popular as they may be but at this point not fully realized include: NATO members promise to ante up 100 bil-lion dollars more (e.g. Germany runs up billions of dollars in Trade Sur-pluses with the US, yet has not anted up her 2% for NATO.); drawing blood from China over its thievery and shameless trade policies; North Korea's cessation of the firing of long range missiles in violation of the airspace of U.S. allies while the Trump administration pressures her to abandon its nuclear arms program.

Other actions by the president remain popular, detested or at least controversial such as: the attempt to rescind Obamacare; disentangling America from the Iran Deal; closing the southern border with a wall; appointing two conservative Supreme Court Justices and many other like-minded judges; opposition to abortion; opening the Arctic Na-tional Wildlife Refuge for drilling; slashing capital gains, corporate and personal income taxes for a wide swath of people; deregulation which led to increased oil, gas and coal production; recognizing Jerusalem as Israel's capital; suspending the nuclear arms agreement with Russia while intensifying sanctions against her; suspending migration from five Muslim majority countries and North Korea and Venezuela; withdrawing America from the Paris climate change agreement.

In his penultimate chapter, "Trump, The Tragic Hero?," Hanson suggests that "Trump's cunning and mercurialness are talents suited to dealing with many of the outlaws of the global frontier such as the Iranian theocracy and Kim Jong-un." Ironically, though, that timely talent may undo him in the long run in the way that Generals George Patton and Curtis Lemay were indispensable to WWII victory yet became dispensable and even caricatures after the war. As Hanson notes while casting Trump for a similar role: the tragic hero willingly faces a societal threat, knowing that this same society may ostracize him after he has destroyed the threat by whatever means. As Hanson soberly concludes: "That is the element of tragedy: no solution, no out in a world of bad and worse choices."

-H/T Terry Scambray

https://www.americanthinker.com/blog/2019/06/victor_davis_hanson_on_emthe_case_for_trumpem.html
Published with permission from the American Thinker.

Is Trump Really Hitler 2.0?

By Mark Deutschle
April 15, 2019

"Was Hitler right-wing? Wikipedia says he was, but does history confirm this? Today's American left would love to be able to assert that Hitler was right-wing in order to bolster the claim that President Trump is Hitler 2.0.

For example, Beto O'Rourke referred to a deceptively edited video that people on the Left claim shows President Trump calling asylum-seekers at the Mexican-American border "animals. In fact, Trump's comment about "animals" was referring to some of the most heinous people on the planet today: members of the MS-13 gang. Then, in case anyone paying attention to his comments was insufficiently provoked, O'Rourke added this: "Now, we would not be surprised if in the Third Reich if other human beings were described as an infestation, as a cockroach, or a pest that you would want to kill, but to do that in 2017 or '18 in the United States of America doesn't make sense."

This is not the first time someone on the left has erroneously accused Trump of Nazi-like tendencies. When Trump spoke about the protests in 2017 that turned violent in Charlottesville, Virginia, he clearly stated a forthright denunciation of the neo-Nazis and their use of violence by saying, "The neo-Nazis and white nationalists ... should be condemned totally." Rather than sharing Trump's comment, most media outlets promulgated the fiction that Trump endorsed the neo-Nazis by repeatedly citing deceptively edited comments. A few days later, giving the media a second chance at getting their facts straight, Trump said, "Racism is evil. And those who cause violence in its name are criminals and thugs, including the KKK, neo-Nazis, white supremacists, and other hate groups that are repugnant to everything we hold dear as Americans."

Unfortunately, the media failed to correct their disingenuous reporting, and thus was born an incident of fake news so notorious that it even garnered its own nickname: the Charlottesville Hoax.

The Left has been calling those on the right Nazis and fascists for a long time. Given the tremendous damage false narratives and specious definitions can cause, it would be helpful to bring forward a clear definition of left and right wing in America today.

Since the right espouses individual rights and limited power for the government, we can examine the historical record to determine if Hitler and the Nazis' rise to power in Germany was built on these ideals. What did Hitler say to persuade Germany that he was the best person to lead their nation? Long before becoming chancellor, Hitler presented his choice of governing philosophies for Germany when he announced his 25 Point Program on February 24, 1920. Let's examine a few of his 25 points to see how they compare to current events in US politics.

> 23. We demand legal opposition to known lies and their promulgation through the press. Publications which are counter to the general good are to be forbidden.

Point 23 of Hitler's program places the state in complete control of the press and hence free speech. In similar fashion, Democrats have shown that they wish to be able to forbid speech they don't like. In 2014, every single Senate Democrat voted for a constitutional amendment that would have given to Congress and the States the power to "regulate and set reasonable limits on the raising and spending of money by candidates and others to influence elections."

> 24. We demand freedom of religion for all religious denominations within the state so long as they do not endanger its existence or oppose the moral senses of the Germanic race. The Party ... is convinced that a lasting recovery of our nation can only

succeed from within on the framework: "THE GOOD OF THE COMMUNITY BEFORE THE GOOD OF THE INDIVIDUAL."

These ALL CAPS were included in the original version by the way, emphatically showing that the citizen was to be totally suborned to the state. Current thinking on the Left regards an individual's free expression of his faith to be allowable only in private. Check with Chick-fil-A and outspoken Christians on college campuses or in Hollywood to gauge the ferocity of abuse likely to come your way for standing up for your beliefs in the public square.

> 7. We demand that the state be charged first with providing
> the opportunity for a livelihood and way of life for the citizens.

The Democrats two months ago released their Green New Deal, which has an overview released by Alexandria Ocasio-Cortez's office stating that it aims to provide "economic security for all who are unable or unwilling to work." Most, if not all, of the Democrats currently running for president have come out in favor of the Green New Deal.

> 17. We demand a land reform suitable to our needs, provision of a law for the free expropriation of land for the purposes of public utility, abolition of taxes on land and prevention of all speculation in land.

The Green New Deal is not bashful about matching Hitler's level of government confiscation, demanding that anyone owning property in America must involve himself in "upgrading all existing buildings in the United States and building new buildings to achieve maximal energy efficiency, water efficiency, safety, affordability, comfort, and durability."

> 25. For the execution of all of this we demand the formation
> of a strong central power in the Reich. Unlimited authority

of the central parliament over the whole Reich and its organizations in general.

Hitler was clear that he was in favor of unlimited authority for his
government. The Democrats' enthusiastic welcome for the Green New
Deal shows that just like Hitler and the Nazis, the left today relentlessly
pushes for the government to gain controlling power over speech, the
economy, health care, energy, our homes, and even our lives.

Fortunately, the right has noticed the Left's growing thirst for power
and continues to fight the expansion of government. For example,
when the government takeover of health care known as Obamacare was
passed by Democrats in Congress using questionable parliamentary tactics, Tea Party activists rose up in indignation, costing Democrats 63
seats in the House along with six in the Senate in the next election.

Maybe back then some of us failed to see the Left's pursuit of a totalitarian government evidenced by Obamacare, but America today is
grateful for the wonderfully revelatory document that is the Green
New Deal. It espouses the largest expansion of government ever proposed in America, and has been endorsed by almost every Democrat
running for president.

Neither Hitler nor today's left-wing Democrats ever saw a governmental power-grab they didn't aid and abet. Clearly, Trump isn't and
never has been Hitler 2.0. He and his followers are determined to limit
the reach of government, understanding that if government grows
unchecked, personal freedom and an individual's opportunity to advance himself will gradually disappear. If we continue to allow Americans to flourish and prosper through their own free choices and hard
work, the result will always be America "the shining city on a hill."

–H/T Mark Deutschle

**https://tmp.americanthinker.com/articles/2019/04/is_tru
mp_really_hitler_20.html**
Published with permission from the American Thinker.

PART III
POLICY

Townhall Daily

Trump And Capitalism Is A Winning Combination

Gina Loudon
|Posted: Apr 05, 2019 10:17 AM

Source: AP Photo/Paul Sancya

The opinions expressed by columnists are their own and do not represent the views of Townhall.com.

"America's thriving economy is showing the rest of the world that capitalism remains the most effective economic system known to man.

The U.S. stock market just posted its biggest quarterly gains in a decade, as investors were comforted by the appointment of Trump ally Stephen Moore to the Federal Reserve's Board of Governors. Moore is a tax-cutter who helped write President Trump's broadly successful tax reform, and he's expected to resist calls for the Fed to raise interest rates while the economy continues its recovery from the Great Recession.

This news contrasted with continued global weakness, including disappointing reports on manufacturing in Asia and Europe. In Germany, declining exports have coincided with an economic slowdown in China, which is Germany's largest trading partner.

Meanwhile, Brexit difficulties continue to paralyze the U.K., and the French are still rebelling over President Emmanuel Macron's unforgivable socialist tax hikes. Further depressing the global economy is the lack of growth in Japan, due to weakness in exports and lackluster economic recovery.

Yet, while manufacturing is contracting elsewhere, it continues to expand in the U.S. The Institute for Supply Management's index of national factory activity surged to 55.3 in March, an increase of 1.1 over February, and nearly a full point higher than economists had predicted.

Americans continue to enjoy historically low unemployment across all socioeconomic levels, so much so that other countries are now attempting to revive their own economies with bold, effective, Trumpian corporate tax reductions.

And when Americans are working, their outlook improves. A recent CNN poll found that 71 percent of respondents say the U.S. economy is solid, which is the highest level of economic optimism in 18 years. Most of those surveyed approve of President Trump's economic policies and the poll showed his approval rating has climbed to 42 percent as Americans realize that his capitalist policies are working for them.

In fact, America is one of the only industrialized countries that continues to enjoy strong growth thanks to President Trump's commitment to deregulation and adherence to free-market policies.

It's good news for the Trump economy too that the Fed announced that it will forestall planned interest rate hikes in the near future, removing a major source of economic uncertainty. Plus, Steve Moore's appointment to the Fed will further solidify support for an accommodative monetary policy that works in tandem with the President's pro-growth policies.

Going forward, investors are optimistic that President Trump will continue to push back on socialist policies while giving capitalism the freedom to flourish. It also appears that a trade deal with China is forthcoming, as evidenced by Treasury Secretary Steve Mnuchin's smeeting in China, giving investors further cause for optimism. Less than three years ago, China was pirating U.S. inventions without limit; now we're on the verge of a historic agreement to open up China's markets to free, fair, and reciprocal competition.

President Trump has been an unwavering champion of capitalism in the White House, and the effectiveness of his pro-growth agenda is showing that capitalism is still the surest route to prosperity."

–H/T Gina Loudon

https://townhalldaily.com/article/2019/04/trump_and_capitalism_is_
a_winning _combination
H/T Townhall.com

Trump Makes the Elites Pessimistic on Foreign Trade. Good.

By Peter Skurkiss
March 3, 2019

"A gloom has settled over the American elite on trade and foreign policy. This is good news. Here's why.

The dark clouds started forming during the presidency of Barack Obama. Even though, in a number of ways, Obama was anti-American, forever apologizing for this country and its achievements, his foreign policy was not exactly a globalist's delight. Obama's appointment of the ineffectual Hillary Clinton as secretary of state was a raw political move. When she left, Obama offered John F. Kerry as a sop to the foreign policy blob. Even though Obama was behind international initiatives like the Iran nuclear weapons deal, the Paris Climate Accord, and the overthrow of Gaddafi, overall, he oversaw a retreat, albeit slowly, from the post-WWII consensus.

The 2016 election was a shock to the foreign service community. Hillary was their ideal candidate. In her, the boys from Foggy Bottom knew they could lead the "world's smartest woman" around by the nose with flattery and faux bowing and scraping. Donald Trump, however, was their worst nightmare. This barbarian was uncontrollable and threatened to upend the world as they know it. And worse still, on a personal note, since winning the presidency, Trump has frozen out a great many of his pre-election critics from the plumb government positions they crave.

The inbred blob is infected with groupthink. It acts as if America's destiny were to lead the world forever, no matter the cost. If the American people refuse to shoulder their assigned responsibility to self-sacrifice for the world community, we are lectured that global chaos of biblical proportions will ensue. Part of the reason for the mentality of the foreign service crowd is that since the end of World War II, the U.S. has basically protected and bankrolled much of the world. This is the only environment these people know and are comfortable with. For all of their supposed education and credentials, thinking out of the box is not their forte, even when that box is knee-deep with their failures.

There's another reason why the foreign policy elite cling to the status quo. In his book, *The Hell of Good Intentions: America's Foreign Policy Elite and the Decline of U.S. Primacy*, Stephen Walt writes:

> The busier the U.S. government is abroad, the more jobs there will be for the foreign policy experts, the greater share of the national wealth that will be devoted to addressing global problems, and the greater their potential influence will be. A more restrained foreign policy would give the entire foreign policy community less to do, reduce its status and prominence ... and might even lead to some prominent philanthropies to devote less money to these topics. In this sense, liberal hegemony and unceasing global activism constitutes a full-employment strategy for the entire foreign policy community.

Yes, naked self-interest motivates many in the blob. To think otherwise is to deny human nature to its members.

So why the gloom in the foreign policy community? It's because those people know that President Trump has changed the dynamics. Under him, America's interests will now be put ahead of the interests of foreign countries. There will be no going back when he leaves office. I offer the thoughts of Eliot Cohen in this regard. If you can get past his overbearing presumptuous attitude and his wrong-headed analysis, savor his pessimism.

> This suggests that Trump's emphasis on putting "America first" is not simply the mistake of a foreign affairs rookie but

an expression of something deeper and more consequential: a permanent shift, among America leaders, away from the dominant postwar conception of U.S. foreign policy.

The more disturbing sign for the future, however, is that although Trump has made nearly every aspect of U.S. foreign policy worse, he is not the sole cause of the United States' increasingly erratic, short sighted, and selfish behavior. He has merely accelerated the trend — that of Washington's retreat from its global responsibilities — that was already developing by the time he took office and will outlast him.

The globalist Cohen concludes by saying:

> Indeed, the erratic "America first" of today's populist right may well be replaced in 2020 or 2024 by a no less erratic "America first" of the populist left.
> Eventually, both may be replaced by an "American first" of the exhausted middle.

So even the Democrats can't be expected to save Cohen's interventionist foreign policy agenda. No matter what, Cohen sees "America first" in our country's future. This is to be celebrated, but Cohen and his ilk treat it like something to be lamented.

On to trade. Alan Blinder of Princeton University is a strong advocate for what he calls free international trade. To Blinder, if factories move out of the U.S. to China, use coolie labor to make products cheaper, then ship them back here tariff-free, hooray. That's free trade in practice, where consumers get a lower prices, and according to economists like Blinder, the consumer is a god who must be appeased.

Blinder's free trade has essentially been in effect for a number of decades now. It is what has hollowed out the Midwest's manufacturing base, throwing millions of Americans out of work and resulting in the stagnation of middle-class wages. Blinder's answer to this social catastrophe is to call on the government to do more to help those hurt by free trade. I suppose 45-year old displaced factory workers should be taught to code or trained to be attendants in assisted living facilities while the costal elite grow richer and richer. And throughout this middle-class destroying process, Professor Blinder is snug and secure in his tenured ivory tower from where he pontificates as to how the rest of the country should operate. As Nassim Nicholas Taleb would say, Blinder has no skin in the game.

Fortunately, President Trump has come along and upended this free trade racket. Even Blinder is seeing that his position is untenable. He cites public opinion polls that come down heavily on the side of U.S. protectionism. He adds:

Maybe the public sees the central goal of an economic system as providing well-paid jobs, not producing cheap goods. If so, the standard case for free trade evaporates.

Maybe? It seems that every other country on the planet behaves that way. Blinder and his fellow elite are secularists to the core. This is why they cannot understand that "man does not live by bread alone." So like Eliot Cohen, Blinder knows that things are not going back to the way they were even when Donald Trump leaves office. "America first" will continue to be the reigning philosophy in foreign policy and trade. This is why these elitists have that hangdog look about them."

-H/T Peter Skurkiss

https://www.americanthinker.com/articles/2019/03/trump_makes_the_elites_pessimistic_on_foreign_trade_good.html
Published with permission from the American Thinker.

American Thinker

'Experts' wrong again: Trump tariffs have not penalized American consumers

By Thomas Lifson
June 16, 2019

"Ever since President Trump started using tariffs as a strategic weapon in restructuring our position in world trade from losing jobs, industries, and whole regions to one of strength across the board including a viable manufacturing sector, our elites discovered a brand new concern for working class Americans. Those "people of Walmart" they normally scorn are doing to be penalized by skyrocketing prices for clothes, appliances , and other consumables because of Trumps tariffs.

Economic theory is great in the abstract, using unassailable logic and fundamental principles grounded in reality. But human beings and their collectivities are complex, and often intervene in the economic sphere for reasons unrelated to the logic of economics.

Thus, the almost universal establishment criticism of President Trump's use of tariffs to force those who exploit us with high tariff and nontariff barriers to our exports into a more reciprocal relationship. His stated goal of moving toward a world in which tariffs are not necessary is widely ignored, and his choice of tariffs as a strategic tool is castigated "protectionism" and worse.

And we're going to suffer, because Orange Man Bad.

Except that we're not suffering, and the data show that simple (-minded) economics predictions have proven false. Import prices have declined, not risen. Sundance at Conservative Tree House writes:

The latest set of statistics from the Bureau of Economic Analysis (BEA) shows all of the professional pundit claims of higher prices on imported goods due to Trump tariffs are simply disconnected from reality. In actuality the year-over-year prices of import products are actually dropping:

Month	IMPORTS			EXPORTS		
	All imports	Fuel imports	Nonfuel imports	All exports	Agri-cultural exports	Non-agricultural exports
2018						
May	0.9	6.1	0.2	0.7	1.6	0.6
June	0.0	2.6	-0.3	0.2	-1.0	0.3
July	-0.1	0.8	-0.2	-0.5	-5.2	0.1
August	-0.4	-2.1	-0.2	-0.1	0.4	-0.2
September	0.1	0.0	0.0	0.0	-1.3	0.2
October	0.5	3.3	0.1	0.5	-0.1	0.5
November	-1.6	-12.2	-0.2	-0.8	1.7	-1.0
December	-1.4	-13.3	0.0	-0.6	3.8	-1.1
2019						
January	0.2	4.6	-0.3	-0.6	-2.1	-0.4
February	1.0	10.2	0.1	® 0.6	0.2	0.7
March	0.6	6.9	-0.2	® 0.8	1.0	0.7
April	® 0.1	® 1.7	-0.1	® 0.1	-1.5	® 0.2
May	-0.3	-1.0	-0.3	-0.2	-1.0	-0.2
May 2017 to 2018	4.5	30.1	1.8	5.0	4.8	4.9
May 2018 to 2019	-1.5	-1.1	-1.4	-0.7	-5.3	-0.2

Footnotes

(source)

U.S. Import prices fell 0.3 percent in May, the first monthly decline since a 1.4-percent drop in December. Import prices advanced 1.8 percent from December to April before the downturn in May. The price index for overall imports decreased 1.5 percent over the past 12 months, matching the drop in January. These were the largest over-the-year declines since the index fell 2.2 percent in August 2016. (See table 1.)

Part of the explanation for this is that China is forced to subsidize exporters in order to maintain employment. Most journalists and academics fail to understand the vulnerability of the Communist regime in China to popular unrest. There are tens of thousands of incidents a year of popular revolt against officials, news of which rarely leaves China. The sole reason that people put up with an autocratic and corrupt political-economic system is that it has delivered increasing levels of prosperity. If that prosperity falters or crashes, watch out.

A second explanation for the powered prices for imports is the lower energy prices that the US oil production boom has provided. That is a weapon that President Trump can take a bow for – by unleashing the incredible productive capacity of our energy industry once the government hobbles are removed. Our elites are insufficiently aware of the contribution it makes to our welfare and strategic strength. They think that Silicon Valley is the sole definition of American technological leadership. They're wrong. The oil and gas industry is at least its equal.

And thus, for reasons that eluded the academics and globalist elites but which apparently Donald Trump had some grasp of, the price for his tariffs is being paid by China and oil exporting countries, not US consumers"

-H/T Thomas Lifson

https://www.americanthinker.com/.../**experts_wrong_again_tru mp_tariffs_ have_not_penalized**_american_consumers.html
Published with permission from the American Thinker.

The Historical Roots of Donald Trump's Foreign Policy

By Avi Berkowitz
October 16, 2018

"Seventy years of post-war diplomacy ruined" is the consensus establishment view of Donald Trump's America First foreign policy. And it is true. But Donald Trump is not the first president in postwar America to rattle the iron cage of establishment diplomacy. That honor goes to Harry Truman, who ruined Franklin Delano Roosevelt's vision of the postwar world when he did what Roosevelt would have never done – drop two nuclear bombs on Japan.

Nor is President Trump the first postwar president to tread in Truman's footsteps. Both Richard Nixon and Ronald Reagan did that before him. And yet, there is clearly something unprecedented in Donald Trump's foreign policy, something akin to a paradigm shift whose roots track back to Richard Nixon's *modus vivendi* with communist China, but whose long arc seems to bend toward our final liberation from the Manichean dualism that has deformed American foreign policy since the day after the bombing of Nagasaki – that is, since the day that America's cultural elite rejected what Harry Truman had created: a world made in America's image.

Richard Nixon secretly engineered the Sino-American rapprochement during the darkest days of the Vietnam War. Its purpose was to stifle the vaunted consequences predicted by the domino theory that would have otherwise ensued from America's military defeat in Vietnam, to which Nixon was resigned. But Nixon also knew that America's rapprochement with China would dislodge Russia from its vanguard position at the head of an irresistible global revolution. Denied its place of privilege, the Soviet superpower would be revealed for what it was: a standard 19th-century Great Power resting upon a territorial empire that was considerably larger than but otherwise indistinguishable from its pre-communist predecessors. Suddenly, and despite its nuclear arsenal, Soviet Russia would look remarkably like its tsarist predecessor, and its policies would quickly mimic those of the old Russian bear. Soon enough, it would become clear that the sleek Soviet boot crushing the "toiling masses" was designed deep in the tsarist hinterland not for the sake of the Revolution, but for the sake of Mother Russia.

By publicly shaking hands with Chairman Mao in "occupied Peiping," President Nixon instantly discredited the cruel logic of global bipolarity and its demonic balance of terror upon which the postwar international system was supposedly based. In retrospect, even the actual history of the world since the bombing of Nagasaki seemed to vindicate a global political order based on something other than the stability inadvertently generated by two "MAD" (Mutual Assured Destruction) superpowers toting nuclear weapons cruelly targeted on each other's civilian populations. That something was America's unchallenged position as the world's one and only superpower.

America's dominance in world affairs was already obvious in the late 1940s, first when the American air bridge neutered the USSR's ill conceived blockade of West Berlin and then when the Soviets tried and failed to defy the Doctrine of Containment by breaching the American monopoly in the Middle East. In the 1950s, America manifested its complete superiority over the Russians when it continued to exclude them from the oil-rich region even after the Suez War. Finally, the lack of polarity between the two "superpowers" was displayed before the entire world in the 1962 Cuban Missile Crisis. The so-called missile gap was never more than a joke by Dr. Strangelove.

But if by playing his China card, Nixon revealed the Cold War to be a colossal house of cards, why didn't he immediately follow up his China triumph with an even more important one in Europe by flying directly from Beijing to Berlin and ordering the Soviets to "tear down this wall"? And, fifteen years later, when "Mister Gorbachev" did exactly that after Ronald Reagan finally demanded it, why did the myth of bipolarity persist?

Although the Soviet Union quickly disintegrated, America did not unveil any new unipolar international political system. Instead, America blundered through thirty years of strategic anomie, beginning with George Bush, Sr.'s cockamamie scheme to build an American global imperium, which he called the New World Order, winding its way through the trials of triangulation in which China was featured as a second communist superpower and culminating in Barack Obama's reckless and unforgivable decision to nuclearize the Islamic Republic of Iran in order to make believe that even without a second superpower, the global balance of terror remained in place.

Apparently, the need to maintain the myth of bipolarity was so strong that successive presidents – Republicans and Democrats alike – have refused to forsake it. My question is why.

My answer is that MAD's mythical pull is hiding inside the historical narrative, albeit never as a political reality, but as a dualistic culture of condominium and conflict between capitalism and Marxism to ensure progress in world affairs.

Let us re-evaluate the world that actually existed at the outset of the postwar years and critically compare it to this Cold War myth. This critique must begin with a clear understanding of the worldview of America's last pre-Cold War president, Franklin Delano Roosevelt, and the defeat of his fossilized vision of world politics, which resulted from the nuclearization of the world.

By the end of his unprecedented third term, Roosevelt knew he was dying. But he ran and won re-election in 1944 anyway, as a prisoner of his megalomania. Roosevelt was convinced that only he and Joseph Stalin had the necessary authority to construct the postwar world.

On April 1, 1945, the Allies arrived at the Elba River with a clear path to Berlin. Instead of marching forward to victory, they rested for six weeks until the Russians arrived from the east because Roosevelt and Stalin had agreed at Yalta in February that they would liberate

Berlin together. Doing so symbolized their joint stewardship over the postwar world. The two great powers' division of Europe would serve as the model for sharing the rest of the world in the tradition of 19th-century European power politics.

On V.E. Day, Franklin D. Roosevelt was already dead, but his body was not yet cold. For this reason, I suspect, Harry Truman accepted the already agreed upon division of postwar Europe. He had not the time or the loyalty of Roosevelt's advisers to design and impose different arrangements. But President Truman refused to callously divide the rest of the world with a mass murderer, and by so doing, he liberated the world from the fossilized grip of his predecessor, at least politically.

In August of 1945, Harry Truman ordered the bombing of Hiroshima and Nagasaki. By so doing, he rendered Russia redundant to the postwar world order. More importantly, by nuclearizing the world, he also destroyed Roosevelt's 19th-century vision of power politics, consigning what Henry Kissinger famously called "the World Restored" to Europe's faded past.

Having achieved all of that, why did Harry Truman consent to the phony bipolarity that has plagued us ever since? Because, as an accidental president, Truman could do no more than liberate the nation from the trap of 19th-century *real politik* intended by his overbearing patrician predecessor. He succeeded in defeating Roosevelt's political vision, but he had no way to overcome the entrenched culture that Roosevelt represented. Richard Nixon and Ronald Reagan succumbed to the same forces in their lonely victories over the myth of bipolarity.

But on Nov. 8, 2016, all of that was changed when the ultimate outsider was elected president after challenging not just the mortar of bipolarity's structure, but its cultural foundation as well, which Hillary Clinton and her basket of supporters so exquisitely represented. So far, President Trump seems determined to challenge the foreign policy establishment at its sacred Manichean alter, willing to risk impeachment because he seems to understand that clearing the swamp requires two victories, one political and the other cultural. Only then will America's global destiny as the world's only superpower without imperial ambitions that it actually has been since 1945 become manifest, making the world a safer and better place."

-H/T **Avi Berkowitz**

https://www.americanthinker.com/.../the_**historical_roots_of_do nald_trumps_ foreign_policy**.html
Published with permission from the American Thinker.

Trump Rejects Globalism

By E. Jeffrey Ludwig
February 18, 2019

"Dan Balz, chief correspondent for the Washington Post, has written a powerful screed against President Donald Trump wherein he repudiates Trump's declaration of a national emergency. He expresses in word and tone his hatred and contempt for Trump the man. Sadly, he, along with most Democrats and some Republicans, has qualms about Trump's "national emergency." With compressed lips, they express fears about there being an assault on separation of powers. Or they insist his motive is not national defense, but mere egotistical self-assertion. The many betrayers of the precious soil of the USA offer rank, impromptu renditions of their theme song, called "Besmirch Trump," but in the end, their own inadequacies are on display.

Actually, Balz's animus, and that of the arrayed MSM anti-Trump contingent, is due to Trump's incessant campaign against the agenda of the globalists both here and abroad. President Trump's insistence on the integrity of the American nation-state is profoundly at odds with the globalist mindset, which has taken over the minds and worldviews of many of those in positions of political power as well as the MSM and many of the technology gurus of Silicon Valley. His outspoken desire to improve our border security as well as to defend against Islamic terrorism is causing the apostles of globalism to react in rage against both the man and his policies. I see not only a "derangement syndrome," but a paranoia and extraordinary flight from reality.

One aspect of this campaign against the globalists is Trump's ability, both during his campaign and during his presidency, to look beyond individual accomplishments and likeability of various Americans who are Muslim. Policy issues and likeability quotients of people are two different dimensions of existence and must be addressed differently. Only President Trump took it upon himself to openly and without malice take on this difference, and to express concern about the radical jihadist nature of a percentage of Muslims in the world, and he openly stated that this issue should be addressed in American society before we go the way of Europe. Even when he spoke in Saudi Arabia, he had the courage to denounce jihadism.

The open-door policies of the Left and the weak, go-along accommodation of more conservative elements have enabled unconscionably large numbers of citizens of Islamic countries to move into Europe. This *hijrah* or flood of Islamic immigrants is clearly a Trojan horse operation — an invasion, as has sometimes been stated — with "seeking a better life" as a cover for "seeking a violent takeover." Most are welfare recipients. Their communities are often so hostile to the laws of the countries where they reside that "no go" zones for non-Muslims, even police, exist in England, France, Belgium, Sweden, and other countries. Native-born non-Muslim women have been attacked in unacceptable numbers by immigrants from the Middle East and Africa.

Why do European countries hold these policies? Answer: The Left has a history of being against the nation-state concept. Remember one of their original slogans, "Workers of the World Unite"? The ideal and idea of workers united across nation-state identities would to their minds become the basis of a new internationalism, where control of the means of production would be taken by workers with common interests — whether they be in Russia, Peru, France, or the Congo. This fantasy was never even close to being realized, but it's an ever burning flame in the hearts of the Left. President Trump clearly does not want to see the European experience vis-à-vis Islamist immigration repeated here.

Our relations with Islam and with Islamic immigration are only one dimension of our need to regain our identity as a nation-state, a nation-state that saved liberty and justice twice in the twentieth century. Also by our protracted Cold War against communism (of which many of our young people have little knowledge or understanding), the values of liberty and justice for all were preserved, however imperfectly, from the murderous control freaks of the USSR and the People's Republic of China. Another dimension is the systematic deterioration of our controls over immigration to our country, particularly at our southern border.

The porous southern border poses a different sort of threat to culture from Islamic jihadism. As with unwillingness to have a fully engaged discussion of the dangers of the excessive presence of illegals, the Left wants to exploit this for its own advantage. Leftists want to have these folks come in and vote for Democratic candidates. They want the violence to help de-stabilize our prosperity and security and send a message to the people that America the beautiful is not beautiful anymore. They want to destabilize society in order to effect change, change away from capitalist and toward socialist-communist values (government must grow when there is widespread crime and social disorder), and they want a society where the welfare state is the model of what caring and love look like. (The welfare state model of values and goodness is quite different from the image of peace, charity, love, and goodness advanced by the Bible.)

Trump has dared to challenge this globalist vision that has been growing for decades. He has challenged this alliance at its heart, and sixty-two million Americans realized in November 2016 — however vaguely — that the patriots, lovers of America's history, of our traditions, of Judeo-Christian morality, and of family life, needed to turn back the clock in order to go forward successfully in time and space. **The momentum of the past few decades away from our national unity and consciousness has increased exponentially in recent years. Our prosperity, our identity as one country under God, as well as heirs to a tradition of personal autonomy and responsibility, can continue only if we re-affirm our historic, abiding appreciation for the nation-state concept** — fifty stars on a field of blue emblazoned on the upper left corner of thirteen red and white stripes. Trump was our choice. **Little did**

we know how effective he would be in challenging the globalist status quo.

Despite differences among various factions on the Left, they have in common their desire to ally not with the underdog, as they profess, but with the unstable, disruptive, dependent, and profoundly anti-American elements in our world. In this way, they hope to increase dependence upon big government for security, jobs, education, health, transportation, homes, and energy. **President Trump sees through this power-mad vision that is at its core un-American. This is why we must continue to support his attempt to build a wall, control our border, and stay strong in the face of criminals crossing our borders and Islamic de-stabilizing attempts."**

–H/T E. Jeffrey Ludwig

https://www.americanthinker.com/.../**trumps_national_emergency_draws_fire _because_he_rejects_globalism**.html
Published with permission from the American Thinker.

Trump, Socialism, and the Jews

By Alexander G. Markovsky
August 24, 2018

"Winston Churchill called Jews "the most formidable and the most re-markable race, which has ever appeared in the world." As a Jew, I am perplexed by the Jews' remarkably irrational commitment to the Democratic Party and their formidable opposition to Donald Trump.

The old saw, "There are two types of Jews: those who believe that Judaism is about social justice and those who know Hebrew," contains more than a kernel of truth. By and large, orthodox Jews voted for Trump in 2016, showing superior foresight.

Domestically, as the Trump economic policies are producing prosperity and economic dynamism, Jews benefit just as the rest of Americans and arguably more. Internationally, Trump has proven to be an unabashed supporter of Israel; he terminated the Iranian nuclear deal, moved the U.S. embassy to Jerusalem, persuaded Saudi Arabia to cooperate with Israel against Iran, and broke the back of the Palestinian Authority. He destroyed ISIS and supplied Israel with the most sophisticated weaponry in the American arsenal. Incredibly, he has accomplished all of this in his first 18 months in office. No American president has done for Israel so much in such a short period of time. As a matter of record, with the exception of President Richard Nixon, no president has done for Jews and Israel so much, period.

A vast majority of American Jews remain unimpressed. They are not motivated by concerns for Israel; they are not motivated by the interests of the United States and are eminently not practical about their own necessities. What they all passionately care about is social justice. Social justice, in terms of helping the sick and the poor, is deeply embedded in Judaism; for Jews, it is a case of irrational obsession. With the emergence of the industrial revolution and massive generation of wealth, Jews took up economic inequality and embraced ideas of socialism.

The Jewish love affair with socialism which began in Russia with the fanaticism of the grandparents has been transformed into the fear of the parents and subsequently into the conviction of the children and grandchildren; it is embedded deeply in the Jewish DNA.

Living in ghettos for two millennia, the Jewish people have been struggling to reconcile their tragic history with the logic of modern reality. They have a difficult time coming to terms with the freedom and equal opportunities that America offers. They continue to fight for social justice, refusing to recognize that, as far as Jews are concerned, what they have accomplished in this country goes well beyond their wildest expectations. Sons and daughters of the first immigrants, who dug trenches and washed dishes in New York, became doctors, lawyers, senators, bankers, and industrialists.

Unfortunately, the descendants of the first immigrants inherited the genetic memories of their ghetto ancestors. They feel guilty for achieving a standard of living as good as or better than any other ethnic group in this country. The guilt associated with their own success has led them to take on, and support, the cause of every underdog and liberal and socialist movement in sight, no matter how undeserving, no matter how irrational.

Although socialism brought terrible suffering to Jews, they would not abandon their devotion to the cause. As prominent Zionist Zev Jabotinsky once said, "logic is an art of the Greeks; a Jew has his own logic. Jewish logic is the logic of catastrophe. Jews do not detect danger; they face it when it comes."

But history punishes willful blindness, and catastrophes keep reappearing.

In many ways, the 1917 socialist revolution in Russia was in fact a Jewish revolution. Jews founded and shaped the Soviet state. Yet these same Jewish Bolsheviks quickly became the first state's victims. Over the next twenty years, by 1937, practically all of them were executed or murdered abroad.

In the late 1920s, some German Jews voted for Hitler's National Socialist Party, only to become victims of the Holocaust a decade later. They chose to ignore Hitler's anti-Semitic rhetoric; he could not be bad, much less evil. After all, he was a socialist!

Jews passionately supported and continue to admire Franklin D. Roosevelt, who in 1939 denied entry for Jews seeking asylum from Nazi extermination and sent them back to the concentration camps. Nevertheless, Jews voted for FDR and still love him – after all, the New Deal was a giant step toward socialism.

In our own time, Jews continue to ignore the teachings of Karl Marx, their fellow member of the tribe, that socialism is about redistribution of wealth. The aim is to take it from the rich, even though there are many Jews among them. This is what Bernie Sanders's suicidal "Future to Believe In" is about.

What is really remarkable is that over the last century, no social macrocosm has more consistently voted against its own self-interest and survival. We may expose Jewish devotion to socialism and shame Jews for betraying their own interests; however, conviction is stronger than reason.

As the leadership of the Democratic Party dropped all pretenses and openly advocates socialism in this country, the heritable socialists impelled by conviction will ignore once again the political necessities and vote for the party that speaks their language."

-H/T Alexander G. Markovsky is a senior fellow at the London Center for Policy Research and author of **Anatomy of a Bolshevik** *and* **Liberal Bolshevism: America Did Not Defeat Communism, She Adopted It.**

https://www.americanthinker.com/articles/2018/08/trump_socialism_and_the_jews.html
Published with permission from the American Thinker.

Trump and the Jihadis

By Alexander G. Markovsky
January 4, 2019

"Once again, President Trump exhibited the leadership and courage in challenging the accepted postulates and ignoring established rules and precedents. The unwavering sense of the national interest led him to reconsider previous commitments to Afghanistan, Syria, and possibly Iraq. After almost a generation of fighting in the so-called a "war on terror," with trillions of dollars spent and thousands of Americans dead and wounded, the questions are: are we better off now than we were seventeen years ago when the war began? Are the countries we engaged in better off today?

Not so long ago ISIS was marching in unrelenting waves of religious acclamation and territorial expansion accompanied by terrorism and atrocities the world has not seen since World War II. When Trump during the 2016 election campaign promised to destroy the caliphate "very quickly", he was mercilessly ridiculed by his opponents and the media. In less than two years, Trump decimated the caliphate, cleared 99% of the territory and killed thousands of fighters.

Nevertheless, despite this astonishing success, it would be utterly naïve to expect that the Jihadi fanatics, who adopted an apocalyptic vision of the world and yearn for death, would cease perennial warfare and became productive citizens.

In this war, America and the Western world are facing a type of peril they have never faced before. The immutable fact is that radical Islam is not just a religion; it is also a political totalitarian movement, just like communism and fascism. The movement embraces religious supremacy and a Marxist-type utopian/egalitarian standard of virtue. However, unlike communism and fascism, which were adopted by countries that could be defeated militarily, radical Islam is not a country; this mass movement represented by multiple groups is sustained by an ideology embodied in unlimited human resources around the globe.

Another critical distinction is that this war also challenges the conventional definition of victory. In a conventional war the army loses if it does not win; in the war on terrorism, terrorism wins if it does not lose. And it does not lose, because it has nothing to lose; the purpose of terrorism is not to win but to terrorize, to break the will and paralyze the society into submission.

Hence, diplomatic solutions cannot be found, nor is it possible to defeat it in strictly military terms.

In order to face up to the enemy, we must recognize that the war with radical Islam is not just a military confrontation; it is also an ideological and a political affair. First and foremost, this monster has to be defeated ideologically by superior principles advanced by Islam itself.

And, it is not a "mission impossible." Some Muslim leaders are awakening to the realization that violence will not turn the clock, which the Arabs have invented, back to their greatness. They find support among the majority of Muslims who adhere to a peaceful and pluralistic interpretation of their faith. Indeed, Egyptian President Abdel Fattah el-Sisi has denounced Islamic terrorism and challenged religious clerics and scholars to "revolutionize the religion" and bring it in line with Western morality.

In his inspiring yet direct speech during his visit to Saudi Arabia in May 2017, Trump emphasized the both countries' common interest in charting a constructive outcome. He offered Saudis, who spent billions spreading Islamic extremism across the globe, a choice; they had to decide whether they are a country respected by the world community or a cause. At an October 2017 conference for international investors, Crown Prince Mohammed responded positively by laying out Saudis new approach to radical Islam, "We want to live a normal life… coexist and contribute to the world... We will not spend the next 30 years of our lives dealing with these destructive ideas."

Trump, on the other hand, is determined not to repeat the strategic blunders of his predecessors. He is replacing fraudulent idealism with efficacy. Trump's *raison d'état* in the relation to the Muslim world — keeping up the torch of international leadership does not mean providing the security shield to the rest of the world; the idealistic goal of removing tyrants and building democratic nations is incompatible with Islam; condemning Islamic radicalism and restraining the dogs of war, militarily if necessary, is in the best national interest of the Muslim World.

In international affairs, solution often leads to a new set of problems. At this juncture, it is impossible to predict how an acceptable outcome can be distilled from the divergent political interests of Syria, Russia, Iran, Iraq, Israel, Turkey, and the Kurds. However, the status quo that requires continued spending of lives and treasury cannot be tolerated by the American people."

-H/T Alexander G. Markovsky
is a senior fellow at the London Center for Policy Research, a conservative think hosted at King's College, New York

https://www.americanthinker.com/articles/2019/01/trump_and_the_j ihadis.html

Published with permission from the American Thinker.

PART IV:
POLITICS

No collusion, no obstruction

By J. Marsolo
March 25, 2019

"Attorney General Barr has summarized Robert Mueller's report: no collusion, collaboration, conspiracy, or whatever term the Hate Trump media chooses to use, between Russia and the Trump campaign. We knew this before Mueller wasted 40 million dollars. But Mueller threw a desperate bone to the media and to the Nadler- Schiff Democrats.

Mueller refused to conclude as to whether Trump obstructed justice. This was a cowardly act to allow the Dems and the media to say, as they are saying, that Mueller did not exonerate Trump on the obstruction charge. Trump, like every American, is presumed innocent unless convicted. He does not need Mueller's Obama-Hillary lawyers to "exonerate" him.

Presumably, the obstruction of justice is firing James Comey, also known as "St. James." There is no evidence that the multitude of investigations of President Trump were affected in any way by firing Comey. In fact, the investigations were more rigorous because Trump fired Comey.

The Democrats, led by Crooked Hillary, wanted Comey fired after he reopened the investigation of Hillary in October 2016. But when Trump fired Comey...that was something else again.

Mueller and his staff of 19 attorneys knew that if they did not reach a conclusion on the obstruction of justice allegation to exonerate President Trump, then the attorney general would have to do so. Give A.G. Barr and Rod Rosenstein credit for stepping up to do the job that Mueller refused to do.

A.G. Barr's letter reads:

> After making a "thorough factual investigation" into these mat-
> ters, the Special Counsel considered whether to evaluate the con-
> duct under Department standards governing prosecution and
> declination decisions but ultimately determined not to make a
> traditional prosecutorial judgment. The Special Counsel there-
> fore did not draw a conclusion — one way or the other — as to
> whether the examined conduct constituted obstruction[.] ...
>
> The Special Counsel's decision to describe the facts of his
> obstruction investigation without reaching any legal conclu-
> sions leaves it to the Attorney General to determine whether
> the conduct described in the report constitutes a crime. Over
> the course of the investigation, the Special Counsel's office en-
> gaged in discussions with certain Department officials regard-
> ing many of the legal and factual matters at issue in the Special
> Counsel's obstruction investigation. After reviewing the Special
> Counsel's final report on these issues; consulting with Depart-
> ment officials, including the Office of Legal Counsel; and ap-
> plying the principles of federal prosecution that guide our
> charging decisions, Deputy Attorney General Rod Rosenstein
> and I have concluded that the evidence developed during the
> Special Counsel's investigation is not sufficient to establish that
> the President committed an obstruction-of-justice offense. Our
> determination was made without regard to, and is not based
> on, the constitutional considerations that surround the indict-
> ment and criminal prosecution of a sitting president[.] ...
>
> In making this determination, we noted that the Special
> Counsel recognized that "the evidence does not establish
> that the President was involved in an underlying crime re-
> lated to Russian election interference," and that, while not
> determinative, the absence of such evidence bears upon the
> President's intent with respect to obstruction."

The Mueller report can and should be summarized thus: there was no collusion, and there was no obstruction of justice. We spent 40 million dollars and two years to learn what we knew before Mueller was appointed"

-H/T J. Marsolo.

https://www.americanthinker.com/.../no_collusion_no_obstruction.html
Published with permission from the American Thinker.

Trump's Righteous Indignation over His Innocence

By Brian C. Joondeph
April 24, 2019

"The American judicial system, based on British Common Law, presumes accused people innocent until they are proven guilty. The burden is on the accuser or prosecutor to prove guilt, rather than mandating the accused prove their innocence.

English jurist William Blackstone described it this way, as has now been coined Blackstone's Ratio, "Better that ten guilty persons escape, than that one innocent suffer." In other words, the greater wrong is that an innocent person be wrongly convicted, rather than vice versa, hence "innocent until proven guilty."

Those wrongly accused or convicted are righteously indignant and outraged over losing their freedom or reputation unjustly, particularly if prosecuted maliciously. And most fight back. President Donald Trump is the latest example of such judicial malfeasance.

The original mandate for the Special Counsel was to investigate, "Any links and/or coordination between the Russian government and individuals associated with the campaign of President Donald Trump."

Despite two years of assurances from Democrats and the media that there were "mountains of evidence of collusion," and despite an extensive and partisan exam of Trump and everyone in his sphere, that portion of Robert Mueller's report came up empty. No collusion.

The second part of his report dealt with potential obstruction, and that portion, despite reading like Joe Scarborough's or Brian Stelter's Twitter feed, also came up empty. They made a point to say Trump was not exonerated, but that's not the standard of American jurisprudence. Trump is either guilty of obstruction or he is not.

The OJ Simpson jury didn't *exonerate* OJ; instead they found that he was not guilty beyond a reasonable doubt. Innocent or guilty is a binary choice. Any doubt, reasonable or not, is enough to invoke Blackstone's Ratio. Is there any reasonable doubt that if Mueller and his team found something, anything, with which to indict Trump, his family, or anyone close to him they would have put on page one of their 400-page report?

Their case for possible obstruction is President Trump's righteous indignation over being falsely accused, this accusation hanging over and crippling his first two years in the White House, preventing him from implementing his agenda. And it went beyond simply a false accusation.

As we are learning, and as will unfold in the upcoming weeks, this entire affair was planned and orchestrated by the Obama justice and intelligence agencies. They attempted to plant spies in the Trump campaign, entrapping those already working for Trump, selectively leaking to the media, then using unverified political opposition research combined with media reports based on leaked information to fraudulently obtain FISA warrants to spy on Trump and his campaign.

More than just being falsely accused, this was a coup against a lawfully elected president, perpetuated by co-conspirators in the media and Congress. Is there any wonder why Trump was outraged? He had just won an improbable election to the presidency, against all odds, outfunded, with almost the entire media against him. And here was an unelected group of partisans trying to take it all away from him.

Who could he complain to? Media coverage was over 90 percent negative. Most elected officials in his party were against him, hoping the allegations were true and that Trump would soon be gone. Despite Trump's conservative agenda, those who once shared such conservatism, like Bill Kristol and George Will, turned on a dime and became Democrats, piling on to the Trump vitriol express.

So, Trump turned to Twitter, his only outlet as the media stood in firm opposition to him. He criticized the investigations as "a witch hunt." He wished he could fire Mueller, even supposedly asking staff to do so, which they did not do. He correctly realized and said, "I'm f***ed", not out of guilt but instead with the realization that his presidency would be paralyzed with the investigation hanging over him. Which it was.

And it was. How many foreign leaders, believing CNN's endless panels of "experts," thought Trump would resign or be impeached? Why make trade or other agreements with an administration about to be replaced? How many Republican Congressmen chose not to run for reelection to avoid being tarred with the Trump collusion scandal that would bring down his presidency and limit their post-Congressional private sector opportunities? Rather than repealing Obamacare or funding the wall, they believed MSNBC's assurances that Trump and his family were soon heading to prison. Would the GOP have lost the House if those who hated Trump and wanted to avoid his stink, like Paul Ryan, stayed and fought alongside him?

Is there any wonder Trump fought back — ferociously as he always does? Was that obstruction or righteous indignation and anger?

Tiger Woods, like Donald Trump, was an unlikely winner a few weeks ago in a contest that no one thought he could win. Suppose Tiger was accused of cheating at the Masters, based on manufactured evidence and doctored videos, and his green jacket taken away from him. Wouldn't he be appropriately outraged and screaming from the rooftops about it?

How about Justice Kavanaugh and the bogus allegations leveled against him? Was his tearful and passionate response somehow obstructing the investigations and Senate hearing? Or was it the genuine heartfelt defense of someone falsely maligned and accused?

Mueller and team performed a neat trick. They pretended to investigate the false claim of Trump-Russia collusion based on the Steele Dossier, known to be bogus even before Mueller was appointed, dragged it out with the assistance of the media, crippled Trump's presidency. Then, when he fires back defending himself, they claim he is obstructing their investigation. Demand Trump had to prove a negative, and when he couldn't and reacted as anyone else falsely accused would act, claimed he was obstructing. Very clever.

Yet Trump did anything but obstruct. As AG William Barr explained in his summary remarks

> President Trump faced an unprecedented situation. As he entered into office, and sought to perform his responsibilities as President, federal agents and prosecutors were scrutinizing his conduct before and after taking office, and the conduct of some of his associates. At the same time, there was relentless speculation in the news media about the President's personal culpability. Yet, as he said from the beginning, there was in fact no collusion. And as the Special Counsel's report acknowledges, there is substantial evidence to show that the President was frustrated and angered by a sincere belief that the investigation was undermining his presidency, propelled by his political opponents, and fueled by illegal leaks. Nonetheless, the White House fully cooperated with the Special Counsel's investigation, providing unfettered access to campaign and White House documents, directing senior aides to testify freely, and asserting no privilege claims. And at the same time, the President took no act that in fact deprived the Special Counsel of the documents and witnesses necessary to complete his investigation. Apart from whether the acts were obstructive, this evidence of non-corrupt motives weighs heavily against any allegation that the President had a corrupt intent to obstruct the investigation.

No collusion and no obstruction, only the righteous indignation of someone falsely accused and besmirched. Congressional Democrats will bray about impeachment. CNN will wholeheartedly agree. But this isn't over.

As a Trump meme making the rounds on social media says, "Hope you had fun investigating me. Now it's my turn."

-H/T Brian C. Joondeph

https://www.americanthinker.com/articles/2019/04/trumps_right-eous_indignation_over_his_innocence.html
Published with permission from the American Thinker.

The Vainglorious NeverTrumpers

By Brian C. Joondeph
March 28, 2019

Vainglorious is a rich, multi-syllabic word that actually describes something well, unlike the similar big words the left uses to confuse and obscure their social justice agenda, such as intersectionality. Vainglorious means to be boastfully vain and proud of oneself, or ostentatious. Shuffle the word a bit and find that it describes someone gloriously vain.

What a great term to describe NeverTrumpers! They are smug in the certainty and righteousness of opposing President Donald Trump and his agenda. They happily point it out every chance they get, whether on a CNN panel or on Twitter, as they look down their proud beaks on those who support Trump.

Never mind that most NeverTrumpers are or were members of the Republican Party, and that most Trump supporters are Republican. They view Trump and his fans as lepers, unworthy to breathe the same rarefied air as the woke NeverTrumpers who see through the Trumpian smoke and mirrors.

Trump is a charlatan, they say, destroying the conservative movement and the Republican Party. This must mean that everything NeverTrumpers have been advocating for on the pages of the late Weekly Standard or the Wall Street Journal op-ed page, like conservative judges, lower taxes, fewer regulations, immigration reform, better international trade deals, and fewer foreign military entanglements, are part of the charade. Perhaps it has all been talk, without principle or conviction.

NeverTrumpers have the closest thing to their hero Ronald Reagan in a generation and couldn't be more unhappy. You know the names

– Bill Kristol, Max Boot, George Will, Bret Stephens, Jennifer Rubin, and Peggy Noonan to name a few. Add to that list Michael Gerson, a speechwriter in the George W. Bush administration, a former senior fellow at the Council on Foreign Relations, and a current Washington Post columnist. He has the perfect pedigree as a Washington, DC establishment insider.

His recent column asked, "Why should a Republican stay in a party that has gone off the moral rails?" Let's unpack his piece.

He asks, "Would being a GOP legislator in the Trump era involve too many sacrifices of principle?" He goes on to say, "And it is not possible in much of the country for a Republican to run and win as an anti-Trump candidate. Even Mitt Romney had to pull back from his criticisms of President Trump to win a Senate seat."

Poor Mitt Romney, who had to run as a self-described "severely conservative" governor of Massachusetts in order to secure the GOP nomination in 2012, only to choke and squander a winnable election, giving America a second term of Barack Obama. How did that work out for conservative principles?

Romney's predecessor, another presidential loser, John McCain, also had a habit of running as a conservative and governing as anything but. McCain also had a prominent role in the Russian collusion hoax, passing the phony dossier to the FBI. Those two NeverTrump Republicans, in the eyes of the NeverTrumpers, were principled, despite being losers and relegated to the back bench of national politics.

Instead their "principled" presidential runs culminated in legalized post-birth abortion, given a standing ovation in New York after Governor Andrew Cuomo signed infanticide into law. Virginia Governor "Coonman" Northam defended infanticide with nary a peep from the GOP smart set about *which* political party has "gone off the moral rails."

What other principles have been sacrificed? Elementary school children are encouraged to cross dress and learn about the 70 something genders, which they are encouraged to explore. Any objection from NeverTrumpers? Who has "gone off the moral rails"?

Religious freedom is tossed out the window if one happens to be a Christian baker, standing on principle, not creating a same-sex wedding cake. Yet if a Muslim baker chose to do the same, and anyone dared criticize this, they would be labeled a racist and hater. Any critic's freedom of speech on social media platforms would disappear, as a matter of principle. Yet NeverTrumpers think it's Trump who has "gone off the moral rails."

The principle of a sovereign nation with a border is racist and xenophobic, while giving illegal immigrants US taxpayer dollars and societal advantages are principles seemingly acceptable to the NeverTrumpers. Allowing criminal aliens free run of our cities, committing murder and mayhem, is acceptable based on some principle of tolerance or diversity. Yet it's Trump who has "gone off the moral rails."

The principle of a fair and honest election has been replaced by the outgoing administration weaponizing its intelligence and judicial agencies to subvert the will of the people with little pushback from NeverTrumpers. The principle of allowing "we the people" to select their leaders and expect such leaders to follow the will of the people is a principle alien to the elites. Yep, Trump is the one "off the moral rails."

Donald Trump is the only one in the Republican Party pushing back against America's slide into the abyss of socialism or worse. He has a simple principle, "Make America Great Again," unambiguous and without nuance. None of the other 17 GOP candidates could have beaten the Obama-Clinton machine and withstood the relentless daily media onslaught every day of their presidency.

It's the Republican Party that has tossed principle to the wind and has "gone off the moral rails." Despite controlling Congress for two years, they accomplished little other than a corporate tax cut. Obamacare wasn't repealed, Planned Parenthood was funded, and the border wasn't secured, despite principled campaign promises to the contrary.

Without candidate Trump, we would have had another President Clinton, the outcome most of the NeverTrump Republicans preferred. How exactly would that have advanced the "principles" they purportedly support?

Imagine if NeverTrumpers put aside their slights for their chosen candidate, whether Jeb! or the mailman's son, not winning the nomination, and got behind their party's nominee? Suppose Senator McCain had chosen to work with his president rather than undermining him at every turn?

Whether or not they liked Trump's style, his MAGA principles were things we have been reading about in the National Review for decades and worthy of full-on support. So much more could have been accomplished. It's a miracle Trump did what he did in his first two years with so few friends and supporters in Washington, DC.

Instead the vainglorious NeverTrumpers have thrown their "principles" to the wind, crossing enemy lines to join the left in opposing the last and only hope of keeping conservative ideas alive, ideas that NeverTrumpers once solidly stood behind. Who has really "gone off the moral rails"? Trump or phony NeverTrump Republicans?

They are beyond despicable. They are throwing the game because they aren't on the starting team, preferring to let the other team win to protect their bruised egos. Now they are in a political wasteland. Trump Republicans want nothing to do with them. Neither do the far-left Democrats.

Their only home is on the op-ed pages of the Washington Post or CNN panel discussions. The glory of it, all for their vanity. "

-H/T Brian C. Joondeph

Brian C. Joondeph, MD, MPS, a Denver based physician and writer. Follow him on Facebook, LinkedIn and Twitter.

https://www.americanthinker.com/articles/2019/03/the_vainglorious_nevertrumpers.html
Published with permission from the American Thinker.

A look at all of Trump's enemies

By Jeff Locke
July 10, 2019

"The legend of Horatius, standing athwart the Pons Sublicius to defend Rome against Etruscan invaders in 508 B.C., is described by Plutarch in his "Life of Publicola," as well as Lord Macauley in "Horatius at the Bridge" (1842). President Trump is today's Horatius, heroically defending us against the foreign invasion.

The president is making a stand against the invaders and those who support them in their effort to overrun the United States. He is outnumbered. Supporting the invasion:

1. **The Democratic Party.** The sanctuary party is blocking urgent legislative immigration reform. Democrats' top priority is to flood the U.S. with millions of illegals, and then, one day, when they control Congress and the White House, declare them all voting citizens. Using the chain migration laws, if each immigrant sponsors ten relatives to be admitted, 30 million illegals legalized yields 300 million new American voters. In the meantime, they intend to nibble around the fringes with assorted voting frauds like DMV and same-day voter registration, liberal mail-in voting, and ballot-harvesting.

Importing a new dependent underclass is part of the Democrats' new DNA. Any attempt at integrity of the ballot is vilified. Any legislative effort to reform immigration is a call to arms for the Left. They even scoff at describing the horde of invaders as a "crisis." They believe that keeping our society in perpetual turmoil and importing a new, dependent underclass works for them politically. Democrats also dishonestly spin the border control issue as anti–Hispanic citizen. Their no-to low-information voters are oblivious.

2. **The Mexican and Central American Governments.** Exporting their "bad hombres," as the president put it, allows them to relieve their social tensions. They add to their national income by having the illegals remit to relatives and friends back home:

> Mexico $25 billion annually (2% of GDP)
> Guatemala $9 billion annually (12% of GDP)
> El Salvador $500 million (21% of GDP)
> Honduras $5 billion (20% of GDP)

Big incentives all around. South of the border, bribes paid to public officials to facilitate human-trafficking grease the wheels. Social services subsidies from U.S. taxpayers allow the aliens to send money home instead of supporting themselves.

3. **The U.S. Chamber of Commerce.** Many of their members prefer cheap illegal alien labor despite civil disorder and higher government expenditures. Many Fortune 500 CEOs are virtue-signaling about illegal immigration, alienating many of their citizen customers in order to support leftist social justice causes.

4. **The Wall Street Journal.** The news division frequently slants stories on border chaos, and the "free flow of labor" zealots on the editorial page have an opinion that can be described as the south end of a northbound

5. **The Leftist News Media.** Anything that advances the cause of the Democratic Party, they can support and provide aggressive media protection. Add in the human interest twist of poor people just trying to live the American dream, and they have an issue worth flogging. They are the stage managers of Democrat-socialist-progressive-leftist causes.

6. **Hollywood.** Anything Trump wants, like enforcing the law, they are against, including the Constitution and the Betsy Ross flag. Like Obama, they believe in American "guilt," that we screwed up the world, and thus the U.S. must make amends by apologizing and redistributing our wealth globally.

7. **The Deep State.** The Lilliputians are on board with anything that advances the party of government, the Democrats.

8. **RINOS.** They salute the Chamber of Commerce and the Kochs in a desire for low-cost labor in industry, plus lower-cost domestic labor (for gardeners and nannies).

9. **Unelected Leftist Democrat Judges.** These political judges sabotage every effort to enforce immigration law.

10. **George Soros and His Open Society Foundation.** At 88, the Davos king of the globalists for open borders (the GOBs) is dealing with a short fuse to abolish borders and nationalism, which he thinks are to blame for the world's problems. Soros is the post-nationalist man of the century.

11. **Left-Wing Think-Tanks and Academia.** These true believers align with the Democrats in importing new Democrat voters in order to acquire more political power. Throw in free or in-state tuition rates for illegals as a bonus.

12. **The Lawyers Guild.** Defending millions of amnesty claims and millions of appeals (at U.S. taxpayer expense) is a definite boost for legal work.

13. **The United Nations.** The world's most corrupt (see the Oil for Food scandal) and useless bureaucrats desire a world without borders with them in charge. Borders and sovereign countries just impede their mission. Their chilling, Orwellian U.N. 2030 agenda calls for world government, and Goal 10: Reduce Inequalities calls for them to "facil-

itate ... migration and mobility of people." Uh huh. These guys need to migrate, too ... to Pyongyang or Caracas.

14. **The pope.** He believes we're all God's children and there should be no borders or walls (except for the Vatican, of course).

15. **Assorted U.S. Industries.** Especially construction, hospitality, and agribusiness. These industries want greater availability of cheap labor to the detriment of American workers.

16. **The Russian and Chinese Governments.** They see any trouble and chaos for the U.S. as a positive for them. They, however, rigorously enforce their own borders.

17. **Jihadis.** The terrorists see an open border as the easy way to infiltrate the U.S. and murder Americans.

18. **Labor Unions.** Unions see opportunities to organize a new group and expand their revenue and influence, like what they have in the Las Vegas hospitality industry. The teacher union favors anything that advances the cause of more government (and multi-lingual instruction).

19. **The Mexican Crime Cartels.** Human-smuggling and sex-trafficking are an annual multi-billion-dollar product line with high gross margins for the drug cartels. They intend to violently defend it.

20. **The Reconquista Movement.** Some Mexican politicians support flooding the southwestern U.S. with Hispanics so that one day they will vote to secede and become part of northern Mexico.

21. **The Illegal Aliens.** Ten to thirty million (?) of them are here now, and hundreds of thousands more are pouring in monthly, some of whom are apprehended, some not. Democrat progressive socialists vigorously oppose even having them counted in the Census, lest we know how big and expensive the problem is. In the June Democrat debates, all the candidates offered up free health care to non-citizens (which they

already get in emergency rooms). A magnet for immigrants or Kryptonite for citizens? The pipeline has been recently expanded to Africa.

Although aggressively opposed by these powerful antagonists, the president is using every legal tool at his disposal to stop the invading horde: building the wall, pressuring complicit governments, enforcing the laws, deportations, and reducing the magnets for illegal immigration. The costs at every level of government are enormous and hidden. President Trump is opposed in all his efforts by these assorted groups, but most citizens and all conservative Republicans are for him. If the party can keep the presidency and the Senate and flip the House in 2020, then Trump will succeed in stopping the invasion. Otherwise, we will be overrun. This is an existential threat to America.

President Trump is reprising the role of Horatius. The citizens of Rome are counting on him. He needs our support. As Macauley put it in his poem:

> Then out spake brave Horatius,
> The Captain of the gate:
> 'To every man upon this earth
> Death cometh soon or late.
> And how can man die better
> Than facing fearful odds
> For the ashes of his fathers
> And the temples of his gods.'"

- H/T Jeff Locke

Enemies of America align with Democrats to defeat Trump in 2020

By Peter Skurkiss
August 24, 2019

"It is often said that politics makes for strange bedfellows. The Democrats, however, are taking that truism to unprecedented levels. Jumping on the Democrat 2020 bandwagon, but careful not to make it too noticeable, are China, Iran, and the globalists.

Media propaganda notwithstanding, the Chinese are getting desperate. President Trump is choking off their oxygen supply, which is trade. The best relief China can get is by the election of pliable U.S. president who, after some kabuki theatrics, will revert to business as usual with them. China's dream president would be Joe Biden. One can only imagine the reams of dirt they have on Slow Joe from their dealings both with him during his vice-presidency days and their shady business arrangements with his wayward son, Hunter.

The other Democratic presidential candidates are not all that bad from China's perspective, either. None have made an issue of either how compromised Biden is regarding China or what Chinese economic aggression has done to the American economy. This is a clear sign that they are soft on China — certainly softer that Donald Trump.

As for Iran, the Trump administration has put the mullahs in a world of hurt. Iran wants nothing more than to have the sanctions removed and get back to the halcyon days of Obama administration when their nuclear ambitions were coddled and their terrorist activity was, if not overlooked, then at least downplayed. To the Iranians, Trump is a bone stuck in their throat. The election of any of the Democratic candidates would be a godsend to them. They would especially like Biden in the Oval Office, since he too pines for the abandoned nuclear deal. Like the Chinese, expect the Iranians to work covertly to see that President Trump is defeated.

Then there are the globalists. They would like to smother U.S. sovereignty with international organizations and multilateral treaties and would render the U.S. Constitution to being a mere historical artifact. Those internationalists have played a major role in damaging the U.S. industrial base to a degree that Hitler, Tojo, Mao, Stalin and the rest could only dream of. Their fingerprints are all over the labor arbitrage that exported U.S. jobs and factories to Third World countries while simultaneously importing massive numbers of immigrants. This diabolical process weakens both the American working class and the cultural core of the country.

Paid shills for the globalist agenda dominate broadcast, cable, and print media. The titans of social media personally find American nationalism repugnant and are willing to place their foreign business interests ahead of America's. In the past three presidential election cycles, the Democratic Party was their party. It will be the same this time only more pronounced.

It is no accident that Democrats dovetail in so smoothly the internal and external enemies of our republic. That party has long since been captured by leftists who despise America's founding, its history, its traditions, and the majority of its people. Hate oozes out of them. To the left, America is so flawed that she must be brought low so as to be transformed into something else. One only has to listen to the twenty or so Democrat candidates to hear that message.

Come election time, no voter — black, brown or white — should be under any illusion as to the exact nature of the Democratic Party. Readers here know the threat the Democrats pose to our constitutional republic."

H/T Peter Skurkiss

https://www.**american**thinker.com/.../**enemies_of_america_alig n_with_ democrats_to_defeat_trump_in_2020**.html
Published with permission from the American Thinker.

Townhall *Daily*

The Oncoming Train

Gil Gutknecht
|Posted: Mar 17, 2019 12:01 AM

The opinions expressed by columnists are their own and do not represent the views of Townhall.com.

The Oncoming Train

"Watching the Jeep Super Bowl commercial several times, it suddenly became clear, President Trump is on his way to a 45 state landslide.

You are way out over your skis, some will say. Get this guy some smelling salts!

What about the nonstop investigations? What about Stormy

Daniels and Robert Mueller? What about the angry Left and their apologists in the national media? What about Mr. Trump's prickly, in your face persona? What about the feckless Congressional Republicans and the never Trumpers? What if the trade talks with the Communist Chinese come up empty?

Watching the Jeep ad, it became crystal clear. None of that really matters. It is just noise.

All elections boil down to fairly simple questions. The next election will not be a matchup between a larger than life Donald Trump and one of the twenty-odd, Left-lurching munchkins. It won't even be a contest between a Republican and a Democrat (Socialist). It will be a contest between those who love this country and those who don't.

It's as simple as that.

The marketing and advertising guys at Jeep understand that here in the land of the free, there is still a majority of us who are patriots. Especially among prospective Jeep buyers. Ask yourself this, how many people share the same distain for our country that most leading Democrats do?

Democrats reinforce this every day.

The Left wants to destroy everything most of us believe in. It wasn't a slip of the tongue when New York Governor Cuomo said that he didn't think America was that great. Like the militant Taliban, they want to tear down the monuments and memorials that a handful of radicals think offensive. To them, our founding was flawed. Our founders were racists slave owners. Christopher Columbus was a criminal. American history is pockmarked with one abuse after another.

Democrats somehow have convinced themselves that most of the problems in the world can be blamed on the United States. Others are poor because we are rich. To them our wealth has nothing to do with free people interacting in a free market. No, it is because we have exploited and stolen from others. They conveniently ignore the enormous price Americans have paid to plant the flag of Liberty around the globe.

They are now willing to openly advance Socialism as the only cure for the inequities of Capitalism. Never mind the overwhelming evidence that raw Socialism goes against human nature and it has never worked…anywhere.

They believe traditional morality is passé. Marriage is outdated. People of faith are only slightly higher than Neanderthals. The Left worships humanism, diversity, the environment and the latest class of victims. Their only sacrament seems to be the sacrificing of the unborn, slaughtering them even after babies are born alive.

It is sick!

The fight over the border wall crystallizes this great divide. The Left has so much contempt for this country that they do not believe we have the right to defend our borders. With the help of fellow-travelers in the media, they torture our language. They turn the arguments on their head convincing some that those who believe in the rule of law and that citizenship remain a precious thing are just mean-spirited. Anyone who disagrees must be shamed and demeaned. Even expressing the view that Western Civilization is worth defending is now branded as hate speech.

Ordinary Americans, the ones who defend this nation and get a little misty watching the Jeep commercial, have had more than enough of the self-righteous, Blame America First crowd. The vitriol that Democrats dispense daily for our country, its values and its history cannot be explained away. Voters see it clearly. They know that the anti-America crowd cannot relate to them, let alone understand how they feel. Donald Trump clearly loves this country and he does relate to them.

Distain for America may be just the ticket to move the Democrat base. Democrats don't see the oncoming train, but they have punched their ticket to electoral disaster in the general election.

You can drive that Jeep to the bank."

-H/T Gil Gutknecht

https://townhalldaily.com/article/the_oncoming_train
H/T Townhall.com

Who Comes after Trump?

By Michael Filozof
March 1, 2019

"Halfway through President Trump's first term in office, the jury is still out on his effectiveness in his quest to "make America great again."

Trump has had some apparent successes: the confirmation of Supreme Court justices Gorsuch and Kavanaugh, the opening of relations and denuclearization talks with North Korea, a national tax cut, and a simplified set of tax deductions.

He has, however, failed to pull the U.S. out of NATO. Though he has announced troop reductions in Afghanistan and Syria, he has not yet ended American involvement in either war. And in his biggest humiliation to date, Trump brazenly promised to shut down the government for "years" if necessary to build the wall on the southern border but capitulated after only weeks.

The fact that Trump was willing to even mention these issues in public — along with his opposition to abortion and gun control — has been a victory of sorts for conservatives, given the alternative.

Until now, the fact that Trump is "not Hillary" has been enough. But it will not be enough forever. If the election of 2016 was the "Flight 93 Election" (as Michael Anton wrote in the Claremont Review of Books under the pseudonym Publius Decius Mus), a vote for Trump was a no-brainer. Had Hillary stormed the cockpit and seized the controls, America as we understood it would have been finished. At this point in his presidency, it might be said that Trump wrestled control of the left seat and has succeeded in keeping the plane stable and level, but it is not clear that he knows how to land it (a possibility Anton admitted in his essay) — and the terrorists are still beating on the cockpit door, trying to break it down.

Trump could lose his grip on the yoke in a number of ways. He could be impeached; he could lose in 2020; he could — God forbid — be the victim of a Deep State plot worse than what the FBI and Department of Justice have already attempted to do to him.

He could be re-elected and serve a second term. But the probability of that happening is hardly guaranteed.

Whatever happens, it is worth asking: "Who comes after Trump?"

We know *what* comes after Trump if the Democrats gain control. The Trump presidency, be it a success or failure in terms of fulfilling his stated campaign promises, has had the salutary effect of unmasking the Democrats.

They have revealed themselves as the party of late-term abortion if not infanticide; the party of using the national security state apparatus to spy on political opponents and attempt to overturn elections; the party of violating attorney-client privilege to get an opponent; the party of radical gays and transgenderism; the party of radical gun control and Australian-style forcible gun confiscation; the party of anti-white racial demagoguery and "reparations" for slavery; the party of hate crime hoaxes; the party of open borders, unlimited immigration, and abolishing Immigration and Customs Enforcement; the party of seventy- to ninety-percent income taxes on the rich; the party of socialized medicine and making private insurance illegal; the party of outlawing all fossil fuels (and eliminating airline travel) within ten years, and the party of telling people not to have children to "save the planet."

In other words, they are the party of unlimited socialist dictatorship — the United States Constitution, the enumerated powers, and the Bill of Rights be damned.

But who comes after Trump on the right, to continue his efforts to stave off the disaster that a Democratic-controlled government will surely bring?

Here, the situation is almost equally grave. To a large extent, Trump is a man without a party. Republican support for Trump has been tepid at best, if not outright hostile. Failed 2012 presidential candidate Mitt Romney's first public act as U.S. senator from Utah was not to call out the baby-killers and the gun-grabbers in the Democratic Party, but rather to disparage Trump. The Republican Party lost its biggest House majority since the 1920s in last year's midterms and barely hung on to the Senate. Speaker Paul Ryan failed to deliver border wall funding for Trump before voluntarily leaving office — the second Republican speaker in a row to simply quit rather than continue the fight. (Contrast that with the indefatigable Nancy Pelosi, who like a vampire rose from the crypt to reclaim the title of speaker after losing it in 2010). The Republicans have proven to be the party of go-along-to-get-along country-clubbers, not political street fighters.

It is, in fact, useful to think of Trump not so much as a Republican, but as if he were a third-party candidate who came out of nowhere and won the presidency to the surprise of both established parties.

The last actual third-party candidate to do that was Lincoln, the first president from the then-upstart Republican Party in 1860. Lincoln's victory put the Whigs out of business forever — but it also sparked the Civil War and ultimately cost him his life. Nonetheless, Lincoln's Republicans went on to national dominance, wining fourteen of eighteen presidential elections between 1860 and 1928.

But it is far from clear that Trump has Lincolnesque coattails. Trump was *sui generis* in 2016. He had money and name recognition, two things needed to succeed in politics. Most candidates need the media and a party to supply those things; Trump didn't. How many other people out there have Trump's notoriety, money, pugilistic attitude, and willingness to take on The System if Trump fails — or is taken out? Who else is willing to sacrifice his own money and public image to the unfathomable abuse the left and the media have heaped upon Trump?

No one that I am aware of. Trump needs to establish a long-term movement and a permanent majority — and it is not certain that he is able to do so. Meanwhile, demographics are steadily favoring a Democratic future.

With Democrats in control of the House, it is evident that Trump's wall to stop illegal immigration will not get built. Nor will *legal* immigration be limited — in fact, Trump is in favor of it. Yet immigration, both legal and illegal, will eventually flip Texas and Florida blue and ensure Democratic hegemony for the foreseeable future.

So the question remains: will the Trump presidency "make America great again," or will it be a temporary stay of execution from what the Democrats have planned the next time they gain power?

The stakes remain as high for 2020 as they were in 2016. Maybe higher.

America itself still hangs in the balance."

-H/T **Michael Filozof**

https://www.americanthinker.com/articles/2019/03/who_comes_after _trump.html
Published with permission from the American Thinker.

American Thinker

Trump in a Landslide: Here's Why

By Dave Ball
September 2, 2019

"How does one know what the voting public thinks?

Once upon a time, long, long ago, public opinion polls may have reflected, however faintly, some generalization of public opinion. For a multitude of reasons, that is no longer true. To demonstrate that point, compare the August 29 Rasmussen poll showing President Trump's approval rating of 47 percent with the Quinnipiac reported approval rating of 38 percent. Even more irrational are the Quinnipiac poll result that whatever is left of Joe Biden would beat Trump 54 percent to 38 percent in a general election and the Economist poll number that asserts that 55 percent of the public thinks the country is headed in the wrong direction. It is a near certainty that none of those numbers reflects reality.

So, discarding the meaningless political polls, I went to the most accurate opinion poll I am aware of for my pre-quadrennial presidential forecast: the Washington County (Pa.) Agricultural Fair.

After my 2016 visit to the fair, I reported that Trump was going to win Washington County big. Why? Enthusiasm was enormous. Trump hats were everywhere. People were wearing Trump shirts and Trump pins. These were not all registered Republicans, either. There was a large booth selling Trump merchandise and doing a land office business. There was no similar Clinton enterprise. The parking lot really told the story. Literally thousands of pickup trucks, gun racks behind the seats, many with Trump stickers and campaign messages on bumpers and tailgates. Mixed in were Mercedes and Lexus, many with similar stickers. If Mercedes and Lexus made gun racks, they would have had those, too.

The County Fair Poll was pretty accurate. Washington County turned out big: nearly 75 percent of its registered voters went to the polls, and they voted for President Trump with 60 percent of the vote. That means a lot of registered Democrats voted for President Trump.

What does the early forecast for 2020 look like based on the 2019 Washington County Fair? It looks as if President Trump will do even better than 2016. I have never seen such enthusiasm, especially so far before an election. More than 75,000 people attended the fair, and the crowd was a sea of MAGA and KAG hats, Trump shirts, Trump pins, you name it. This was Trump country, no doubt about it.

The Washington County Republican Party had a large booth at the fair, as it always does. The booth was a big attraction from morning to night. During the evenings, there were consistently large groups of people at the booth. Some just wanted to talk about how the president's policies were helping their businesses. Others talked about pay raises, still others about how the president was keeping his promises. Results matter to these people, and they are seeing results. Family and country matter to these people, and they see their families and their country better off under President Trump. Many who stopped wanted their picture taken with the "Don and Melania" cutout.

Many wanted to register to vote or to change their registration to Republican. Many of the registrations and changes were twenty-somethings, which is telling. Many others wanted to sign up to work for the party.

If we had Trump signs available, we could have given out a thousand or more to people who wanted to put them in their yards that day. Some 400 people joined the party as active workers. There were two booths this year selling Trump merchandise. In total, this far exceeded what we saw several months before the 2016 election. Imagine what it will be at this time next year.

Across the aisle from us was the Democratic Party booth. It is no exaggeration to say it was mostly empty. There was no enthusiasm or energy on the other side.

President Trump delivers results, and that's what people want. He keeps promises, and that's what people want. He defends our families, our people, and our nation. That's what people want. People simply are not buying the socialist pond scum the Democrats are trying to sell. People want more jobs, not fewer jobs. They want lower taxes, not higher taxes. They want to make their own choices, not have the government run their lives. That's why the Democrats' booth was empty.

Looking around the crowd, the uniform of the day was work boots, jeans, tee-shirts, and ball caps. Those who were not sporting Trump gear were obviously well familiar with John Deere, Kubota, a number of seed companies, Remington, Winchester, the NRA, and John 3:16.

The parking lot was full of pickup trucks because these are working people. They drive America. They are directly impacted by what people at all levels of government do — not in a theoretical or philosophical way, but in a very real way. Government policy and action are, to them, their jobs and their families' security. They work hard, and they expect other people to do the same. They are not looking for handouts or free stuff. They are looking for the opportunity to thrive because they earn it. Many have fought for their country or have relatives who have, and they do not react well to those who disrespect this great nation. They keep their promises and expect the people they elect to do the same. Most importantly, these people vote.

In 2016, the people of Washington County turned out in huge numbers and overwhelmingly voted for President Trump because they like what he promised and believed he would deliver on those promises. The president has delivered on his promises, and people are measurably better off: more people have better jobs; they are more secure; the economy is doing well; and, despite constant Democratic obstruction, progress is being made in many other areas.

The 2019 Washington County Fair is an early poll on how people are reacting to what the president has delivered and how they intend to vote in 2020. The Washington County Fair Poll says President Trump will carry Washington County by a huge majority; what we see here will also be true in many other areas of Pennsylvania. The president will carry Pennsylvania handily. I suspect that the same will be true in many other states." -H/T Dave Ball

Dave Ball is a voice for conservatism, the author of conservative political commentary, a guest on political talk shows, an elected official, and a county party official.

https://www.americanthinker.com/.../**trump_in_a_landslide**_heres _why.html
Published with permission from the American Thinker.

Epilogue/Conclusion

A compilation of profound views and opinions of fellow conservatives, about an extraordinary man fortunately elected president of the USA at the brink of the triumph of disastrous Globalism and invigorated scary Socialism. This tremendous collection of brilliant thought not only boosts our confidence in the Donald, it also is an entertaining read. Every essay depicts all aspects of a solid true down to earth American. How much more could he accomplish if not for the formidable insane resistance. That is why we have to win back the House and fortify the Senate in 2020 with his reelection. Not one vote is dispensable, there can be no room for doubt or procrastination. Our vote is the only weapon that could once and for all slay socialism, communism, globalism, and Islam. Vote as if your life depends on it, for if we lose we lose all hope and our way of life

Remember and keep constantly in mind the Democrats want open borders, illegal aliens, sanctuary cities, Antifa, MS13, Hezbollah, the Muslim brotherhood, taxpayer-funded extreme abortion up until the moment of birth, infanticide, radical gender ideology, toxic masculinity, gun confiscation, 70 percent to 90 percent tax rates, judicial activism, anti-semitism, socialism, communism, globalism, bashing police, disrespecting the flag and avowing the pledge of allegiance, income equality, socialized medicine, and radical environmentalism so-called green new deal, outlawing all fossil fuels. An entire labeled segment of society descended into - **Insanity defined.** Then they call us racists because we eat white rice and buy white eggs.

But President Trump remains hard at work, delivering on the issues Americans actually care about: jobs, tax cuts, higher wages, border security, lower drug prices, a stronger military, and more. It's been three years of real results, and there's much more to come

Keep America Great!

Bibliography

https://www.americanthinker.com/articles/2019/07/the_exceptional_trump.htm

https://www.americanthinker.com/articles/2018/10/the_historical_roots_of_donald_trumps_foreign_policy.html

https://www.americanthinker.com/articles/2019/01/trump_and_the_jihadis.htm

https://www.americanthinker.com/articles/2018/08/trump_socialism_and_the_jews.html

https://www.americanthinker.com/articles/2019/04/trumps_righteous_indignation_over_his_innocence.html

https://www.americanthinker.com/articles/2019/03/the_vainglorious_nevertrumpers.html

https://www.google.com/url?client=internal-uds-cse&cx=016417505616455789357:mttpazkfree&q=https://www.americanthinker.com/author/brian_joondeph/&sa=U&ved=2ahUKEwiSzoGBvb_jAhVKj1QKHfrPAI4QFjABegQIEBAB&usg=AOvVaw1ETQWr8Cf7fouUkJ5EzOsh

https://www.americanthinker.com/author/brian_joondeph/

https://www.americanthinker.com/blog/2019/05/diogenes_search_is_over.html

https://www.americanthinker.com/blog/2019/05/what_do_washington_churchill_and_trump_have_in_common.html

https://www.americanthinker.com/articles/2019/02/president_trumps_sot
u_address_affirmed_liberty_to_unresponsive_subversives.html

https://www.americanthinker.com/author/geoffrey_p_hunt/

https://www.americanthinker.com/articles/2019/04/reminder_trump_is_o
nly_human.html

https://www.americanthinker.com/articles/2019/04/is_trump_really_hitler
_20.html

https://www.americanthinker.com/articles/2019/03/who_comes_after_tru
mp.html

https://www.americanthinker.com/articles/2015/08/donald_trump_and_hi
s_enemies.html

https://www.americanthinker.com/blog/2019/06/trump_the_deviant.html

https://www.americanthinker.com/blog/2019/06/communism_creeps_in_
on_cats_feet.html

https://www.americanthinker.com/blog/2019/06/does_anyone_doubt_tha
t_trump_is_the_emrockyem_of_american_politics.html

https://www.americanthinker.com/blog/2019/05/trump_americas_eagle_s
oars_alone.html

https://www.americanthinker.com/blog/2019/05/trump_is_the_most_lawa
biding_president_ever.html

https://www.americanthinker.com/blog/2019/04/donald_trump_as_the_c
ount_of_monte_cristo.html

https://www.americanthinker.com/articles/2019/03/trump_makes_the_elit
es_pessimistic_on_foreign_trade_good.html

https://www.americanthinker.com/blog/2019/01/trump_our_lincoln.html

https://www.americanthinker.com/blog/2019/03/love_trump_without_ov
erlooking_his_faults.html

https://www.americanthinker.com/blog/2019/06/victor_davis_hanson_on

_emthe_case_for_trumpem.html

https://www.americanthinker.com/blog/2019/03/the_rare_wisdom_of_our_president_is_a_gift.html

https://www.americanthinker.com/blog/2019/07/a_look_at_all_of_trumps_enemies.html

https://www.americanthinker.com/blog/2019/07/trump_as_alexander_the_great_.html

https://townhalldaily .com/article/2019/04/trump_and_capitalism_is_a_winning _combination

https://townhalldaily.com/article/the_oncoming_train

https://townhalldaily.com/article/america's_winston_churchill

https://newsmax.com/article/is_president_trump_the_g.o.a.t.?

https://andy.puzder.com

https://theconservativetreehouse.com (Google: the fundamentals of MAG-Anomics by Sundance)

https://www.ameri**can**thinker.com/.../**what_trump_does_not**_doand_its_ fantastic.html

https://www.americanthinker.com/articles/2019/07/why_trump_matters_to_women.html#ixzz5uHToNkhl

https://tmp.americanthinker.com/articles/.../**trump_is_no_racist**.html

https://townhalldaily.com/article/shock_and_awe_trump_style

https:/townhalldaily.com/article/Jews_and_Blacks_for_Trump

https://www.americanthinker.com/blog/2019/06/**experts_wrong_again_trump_tariffs_have_not_penalized**_american_consumers.htm

https://www.americanthinker.com/.../**trump_in_a_landslide**_heres_why.html

https://www.americanthinker.com/.../no_collusion_no_obstruction.html

https://www.americanthinker.com/.../**is_donald_trump_more_conser-
vative_ than_conservatives**.html

Acknowledgments

Thank you to the great minds of the wonderful worlds of AmericanThinker.com, Townhall.com, The conservative treehouse and Sundance, Newsmax and all of conservative media. Special thanks to Wayne Allyn Root whose article inspired the creation of this book. My appreciation for Dorrance Publishing with its efficiency and comprehensive assistance. Then, of course, Google, MS Word, Adobe PDF, Social media and the Digital universe. Thanks again to the authors whose wisdom made this book a reality.

About the Author

The author is a deplorable normal everyday American who has once been through near-homelessness, near-bankruptcy, food stamps and food banks from which he recovered only because of the freedom that eventually made the opportunity available for him to get back on his two feet. Now contented and grateful for a President preserving, defending and empowering the American dream and way of life, but also becoming apprehensive of disaster lurking in 2020. With no journalistic or literary background he has found this form of authorship a most convenient way to crystallize and embody the fabric of a much needed rare American who can accomplice the enormous and almost desperate task of saving America from the creeps of socialism, communism, globalism, and Islam. His success, however, will rely entirely on the dogged determination of every conservative and sane American to reelect him and win back Congress and fortify the senate. The past three years, he has been an "American Eagle soaring Alone" This time, let us all be a hundred million "relentless" eagles MAKING AMERICA GREAT AGAIN and KEEPING AMERICA GREAT forever.